The
Psychology
of
Reading

The Psychology of Reading

Alan Kennedy

Methuen · London & New York

First published in 1984 by
Methuen & Co. Ltd
11 New Fetter Lane, London EC4P 4EE

Published in the USA by
Methuen & Co.
in association with Methuen, Inc.
733 Third Avenue, New York, NY 10017

Typeset by Nene Phototypesetters Ltd,
Northampton
Printed in Great Britain at the
University Press, Cambridge

British Library Cataloguing in Publication Data

Kennedy, Alan
The psychology of reading.
1. Reading, Psychology of
I. Title
428.4'01'9   BF456.R2

ISBN 0–416–38220–7
ISBN 0–416–35940–X Pbk

Library of Congress Cataloging in Publication Data

Kennedy, Alan, 1939–
The psychology of reading.
Bibliography: p.
Includes index.
1. Reading, Psychology of.
2. Reading (Elementary)
I. Title.
BF456.R2K39   1984   372.4'01'9   84–18984

ISBN 0–416–38220–7
ISBN 0–416–35940–X (pbk.)

Contents

List
of
figures

Acknowledgements

The author and publishers would like to thank the following for permission to reproduce copyright figures:

Academic Press, Inc. for 1.10, 4.2 and 7.2; Acoustical Society of America for 2.2; Dr H. F. Al-Ahmar for 6.2; American Institute of Physics for 2.3; American Psychological Association for 3.6; Bell Telephone Laboratories, Inc. for 2.1; Cambridge University Press for 3.2(c); Dawson Publishing for 3.1(b); Lawrence Erlbaum Associates, Inc. for 7.4; Georgetown University Press for 4.7; Professor R. L. Gregory for 1.6; Harcourt Brace Jovanovich, Inc. for 4.6; Hutchinson Publishing Group for 1.11, 1.12 and 1.13; Professor Dr W. J. M. Levelt for 5.1; Linguistic Society of America for 4.4; The Newberry Library, Chicago, for 3.5(a), (b) and (c); Oxford University Press for 3.5(d); and Reading University Library for 1.9.

Preface

Reading represents a unique challenge to anyone seriously interested in human thought processes. It is an activity that binds together perceptual, memorial and linguistic functions and that, once mastered, allows the minds of two people – reader and writer – to be more intimately joined than any other form of social encounter.

This book is about some of the psychological processes that underlie the practice of reading. Since there are already numerous books available on the subject it is perhaps necessary to offer some kind of justification for adding to their number. The book is meant as an *introduction* to the subject. That is, I hope it can be read by someone with no prior knowledge of psychology. Technical terms have been largely banished and I have attempted to deal with issues on their merits in a direct, but not, I hope, too simple-minded, fashion.

The book treats reading, not as an esoteric 'skill', but as a process which draws on a general human need to find order and meaning in the environment. To establish this point involves, of necessity, ranging widely over a number of issues in the psychology of perception and thought. It should be stressed, however, that it deals with *psychological* processes: the teaching of reading is covered only incidentally. My hope is, none the less, that the questions raised will be of interest to teachers and others concerned with the practice of this mysterious activity.

The book might, I fear, offend some because of the paucity of reference it contains. This was a deliberate and, in the event, extremely taxing decision. Experimental psychologists, possibly more than most, are reluctant to allow an argument to proceed unattended by reference to scholarly authority. The text here has been all but completely purged of such material in the hope that what is said will be thereby more accessible. I am aware of the dangers. In steering a way through many complex issues points of detail have, here and there, been jettisoned and the temptation to qualify arguments has been resisted wherever possible. It is all too easy in such circumstances either to say nothing effectively or to say too much that is wrong. I have tried to avoid both evils.

The book began life as a series of lectures to students of psychology at Monash University, Melbourne. I am grateful to the University of Dundee for its generous provision of sabbatical leave and to the British Council and the Royal Society for financial support. The Economic and Social Research Council and the Medical Research Council provided grants in support of my research, some of which is reported here.

My colleague Alan Wilkes read most of the manuscript and pointed out some obscurity and error. That which remains is, of course, my own responsibility. I owe a great debt to my wife who has spent many hours clarifying issues for me. Mrs Barbara Boyle typed the text and numerous drafts with prodigious speed and accuracy. Finally, I must express my gratitude to M. and Mme Tarrene-Manaut who have provided hospitality for several years, and peace and quiet in which to work.

Eus-sur-Conflent, 1983

Part I
Perceptual factors

1
Writing and speaking

The origins of writing

It is impossible to say when the skills of reading and writing first developed for it is very much a question of definition. Attempts to convey thoughts in pictorial form are as old as the earliest known simple paintings, and we could easily surmise that these were preceded by some less permanent medium; marks scratched in sand perhaps or stones allowed to lie in one particular way rather than another (see Figure 1.1).

The tracks of prey are, to the hunter, a source of information and hence could be said to be unwittingly 'written'. The landscape itself – the profile of a hill or the shape of a group of trees – may come to serve as a signal in as much as elements within it are recognized as signs of familiar territory; and it is a small step from noting some natural feature to providing man-made landmarks in the forms of piles of stones, broken branches, marks on the bark of trees or fires lit as points of reference. These too, in a sense, might be said to comprise

Figure 1.1 An early example of picture writing. This palaeolithic carving is possibly one of the earliest depictions of a scene. It is carved on a piece of antler found at Laugerie Basse, in Auvergne. *Source:* Taylor, I. (1899) *The Alphabet*, vol. I, London: Edward Arnold.

'writing', if by the term we mean no more than some feature in the environment that conveys information from one person to another. But such a general definition of what constitutes writing is not very helpful. There is no sign, for example, that the simple pictures in Figure 1.1 were intended as anything other than representations of *particular* events. If, to satisfy a definition of writing, we demand a degree of *generality* in pictorial representation, so that the same idea is by convention shown by the same picture, this seems in comparison to have been a much more recent intellectual achievement. For example, Figure 1.2 shows a drawing found on the shore of Lake Superior. Five canoes, carrying fifty-one men, went on an expedition lasting three days (three suns). They did well (symbolized by a turtle), rode quickly and were fearless (the eagle). The picture concludes with figures describing force and cunning (a panther and a snake). It is this point, where pictures are employed, agreed between the sender and the receiver as standing for particular ideas, that we might want to mark as the historical origin of reading and writing. What the method and its successors have in common is the desire for a form of communication more durable than speech.

If, as Tallyrand remarked, 'God gave us language that we might conceal our thoughts with speech', it must be admitted that speech itself as a means of communication has one quite severe limitation: both parties to the interaction must physically be present at the same time as the necessary words are uttered. Further, once spoken, the substance of the message is lost and both parties have only memories of what was said. It is difficult

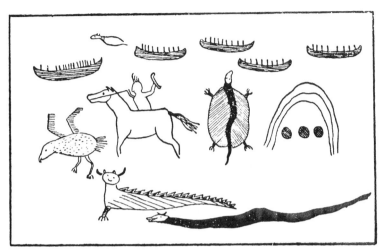

Figure 1.2 A North American rock drawing from Michigan. The drawing describes a successful hunting expedition. *Source:* Schoolcraft, Henry R. (1851) *Historical and Statistical Information, Respecting the History, Condition, and Prospects of the Indian Tribes of the United States,* Part I, Philadelphia.

in our culture, dominated as it is by techniques for preserving the substance of communication, to appreciate the social consequences of relying upon speech alone. One of the most obvious however is the great emphasis in pre-literate cultures on developing techniques for reliably transmitting information verbally from one generation to the next. The 'currency' of this transmission was, of course, the expression of social, cultural, legal and other ideas. The 'medium' was speech itself, but it must not be forgotten that speech is by no means the same thing as thought: it is an event interposed between a stream of conscious awareness and attempts to convey aspects of this to another person. Although its flexibility is very impressive, no one would claim speech as a perfect indicator of thought. Indeed, in some circumstances it is not even particularly good: many of our most significant experiences are, literally, ineffable.

The representation of ideas

These considerations help to clarify several important distinctions that are a necessary part of an adequate definition of writing. As can be seen in Figure 1.3, we may distinguish between two forms of writing, one which is linked more or less directly to the thoughts and ideas of the writer, and the second which is linked indirectly via the medium of speech. In the first case the written tokens passed from one person to another in the form of pictures are intended to effect an exchange of ideas. In

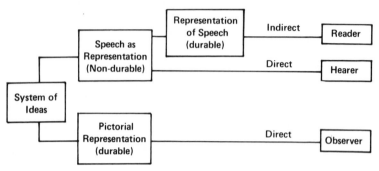

Figure 1.3   Speech, pictures and representations of speech as means of symbolizing ideas.

the second case what is transmitted is at best an indication of what might, in other circumstances, have been *said*. Put this way it may appear paradoxical that the second system (the more indirect) proved to be the more satisfactory, but the reasons for this will soon become apparent. The earliest systems of writing were, in effect, attempts to make durable images of ideas. One might imagine this to be easier for tangible concrete things than for abstract ones. That is, it might seem easier to represent the concept 'table' in this way than the concept 'pride'. However, we should not be misled by this apparent distinction, for to produce pictures at all one must use methods of representation that are conventional to some degree or another. The differences between the images in Figure 1.4 reflect changes, from one culture to another, in what has been thought necessary to set down in order that an observer might have certain predictable thoughts.

E. H. Gombrich (1965, 1982) has analysed the processes that led to changes in the conventions of drawing. He argues that an effective drawing is one which gives rise to a feeling of *recognition*. From this point of view the development of naturalis-

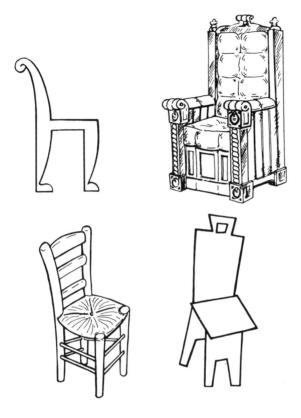

Figure 1.4 Various representations of the concept of a chair. The cultural conventions of Egyptian, medieval and modern society led to changes in the features it was thought necessary to depict and the manner of drawing them.

tic painting can be charted by the discovery of various techniques for arranging lines and colours so that the observer experiences spontaneous, effortless recognition. The discovery of perspective drawing (see Figure 1.5) is one notable example. However, it appears likely that what is taken as an essential defining element in representations of an object changes in time. We may, in fact, now see some representations as clumsy or unnecessarily realistic or, indeed, obscure (see Figure 1.6); but it is fatuous to demand that there be a single, correct form.

Figure 1.5 Principles of perspective drawing. Engraving by William Hogarth, 1754.

Figure 1.6 Early drawing of a piece of electrical equipment in which elements are depicted by means of 'realistic' representations or more abstract forms relating to their function. *Source:* Gregory, R. L. (1970) *The Intelligent Eye*, London: Weidenfeld & Nicolson. (See also graphical conventions used in Figure 2.1.)

Pictographs

There appears to be a continual shift in pictorial representation which makes distinguishing between the banal and the over-stylized a historical rather than a factual judgement. At any time, for a particular culture, there may have been more or less the same variation in the ability of particular representations to give rise to unstrained recognition. It is this very feature perhaps which posed problems for the direct systems of writing illustrated in Figure 1.3. For example, it is possible to represent the human form by a drawing of a 'stick man', illustrating that, for most people in our culture, it is enough to mark the position of the body (though not its shape), and the position and rough extent of the arms and legs for an observer to arrive at a correct interpretation. The overall orientation of the figure on whatever it is drawn can also be used to suggest the position of the person in the 'real world' (e.g. it might be upside down), but it would be a mistake to think of

as a symbol for the *word* 'man' – it is, rather, a representation of an idea. It has its origins, not in speech, but in thought, and represents an attempt to portray the concept of man, a concept obviously so rich as to make this representation very feeble.

Early writing systems of the direct kind used such stylized images – known as pictographs – and the technique developed independently in many civilizations in pre-history. Its obvious and grave disadvantage as a form of writing is that there are far more ideas than the repertoire of simple representative pictures. Even the simplest of concepts is too rich, varied and complex to be pinned down in this way. As a means of communication pictographs are only a marginal improvement on gestures; indeed, many captured abstract concepts indirectly by representing, in conventional form, an appropriate gesture. For example, that the gesture of clasped hands means peace has its explanation in the history of combat and arms. It is a conventional way of displaying, within limits, something about the intentions of the person using it (although clearly gestures could also be used to deceive). A drawing of clasped hands may have developed into a more permanent record of the gesture, and come to mean peace. Pictographs take two possible forms: either a drawing of the salient features of some object, or a more metaphorical representation, as in the case of a drawing of a gesture. In either case these conventional signs are not difficult to read. There is a sense in which such simple pictures are instantly available to convey their meaning since the method of representation is what might be termed 'iconographic'. That is, the relationship between the various features depicted is close enough to the same relationships in the object itself to give rise to instantaneous recognition. Even when greatly simplified, the rules that have been followed are those of graphical convention. Such a method will be effective so long as we agree on the defining features of an object, and these are then presented in an acceptable spatial relationship. In a sense, then, the 'grammar' of pictographic representation is already known to all its potential readers: it is defined by the way the world is seen.

The major drawback to pictographic systems of writing will now be apparent. Such drawings do indeed represent concepts directly in the same way that speech does, but with nothing like the power and flexibility of speech, since they are constrained by attributes of the visual world not really relevant to the process of symbolic communication. There are vastly more nuances of thought than could possibly be captured by pictographic means. To write in such a way is to accept similar constraints to those imposed on the scholars in Swift's fictitious state of Laputa where conversations could only be held by actually transferring objects from one person to another. Even with huge numbers of objects (carried on carts and by overloaded servants) the conversational exchanges possible were ludicrously limited. The solution to this problem is to admit a degree of arbitrary representation; that is, to allow the possibility of symbols that do not *inherently* convey their sense. This could obviously be achieved in various ways, but we shall concentrate here on the development of writing systems that portray speech – an indirect method, but one which, when mastered, gives the same power of expression to the writer as to the speaker.

Phonographic representation

The evolutionary development of language as a 'cloak' for thought was a gigantic step. It endowed *homo sapiens* with the ability to symbolize; that is, to manipulate thought in a manner quite different from the way in which thoughts are generated by the stimulation of the senses. It provided a way of ordering events free, to a degree, from the constraints of time and space existing in the real world. This insight is, indeed, so seductive that at times it is tempting to think of language as primary and thought as its product. *Homo loquens* has what *homo sapiens* lacks, the power not only to attend to and appreciate events in the world, but to create mental representations of these events. In fact the rules of this representational game even allow for the development of representations of language itself. So enormous is the power of this recursive process – an ability to manipulate the tokens of thought – that only very profound reflection allows its limits to be seen. The discovery, therefore, of systems of writing that allow for the depiction of speech marked a fundamental advance: the means of representing a representation of thought.

The invention of phonographic representation appears to have been made independently in at least five ancient writing systems: Sumerian, Egyptian, Cretan, Hittite and Chinese. Whether the form of the invention was identical in all these cases is a matter for speculation, but it is likely that a kind of rebus writing (from the Latin, meaning *by things*) acted in many cases as an intermediate step. For example, the pictograph for an eye, it might be imagined, took the form of a stylized drawing of an eye, but in English the name of the represented object itself, because of its sound, captures a sound in the language (the 'I' sound) which has no connection with 'eyes' at all. Puzzle pictures of the kind familiar to children, such as ram + bull = ramble, are examples of simple rebus writing (see Figure 1.7). Taylor (1899) describes an early example in an inscription of Ptolemy xv:

> we find an amusing instance of a compound phonogram, in which it seems not impossible to detect a faint flavour of Egyptian humour. The name of *lapis lazuli* was *Khesteb*. Now the word *khest* meant to stop and the syllable *teb* denoted a 'pig'. Hence the rebus 'stop-pig' was invented to express graphically the name of *lapis lazuli*, which is figured by the picture of a man stopping a pig by pulling its tail. (p. 59)

Figure 1.7 An example of rebus writing.

Rebus writing comprises a phonographic writing system the unit of which is the syllable. The name of someone – itself an arbitrary designation – is naturally something which the demands of ritual or commerce make it necessary to record. The advantage of a phonographic over a pictographic writing system is very obvious in this case for, unless the individual possesses some very unusual or striking attribute, nothing short of a naturalistic portrait could serve as a representation. Figure 1.8 is an ancient example of phonographic writing: it is an inscription of the name of King Sent and is derived using a sequence of rebus representation which leads to the sound of his name. The Aztecs developed a very similar technique for representing proper names.

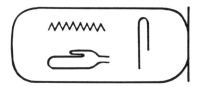

Figure 1.8   Egyptian inscription of the name of King Sent. Described by Taylor as 'the oldest written record in existence' it uses three alphabetic characters. The two on the left are possibly ancestors of our letters 'n' and 'd'. *Source:* Huey, E. (1908) *The Psychology and Pedagogy of Reading*, Cambridge, Mass.: M.I.T. Press.

Logographic representation

It might at this stage be objected that a possible route in the development of writing systems would be for pictographic methods to progress to the point where a unique symbol is used to represent each word in the language. Such 'logographic' writing has often been discussed in the context of ideal writing or ideal language – which we shall consider later – but has never, as far as is known, been developed as a means of communication. The reason is obvious: the number of words in the vocabulary of even poorly educated people is large so that the *arbitrary* assignment of a symbol to each word would represent an intolerable memory load for anyone setting out to master the writing system. The word 'arbitrary' is important, for it could be said that the vocabulary of speech itself represents such a load. There is, after all, nothing about a tree which demands we call it 'tree'. In fact it could just as well be called 'arbre'. However, *this* massive vocabulary of arbitrary designations is, in fact, effortlessly mastered by all normal children. The point is, though, that while the number of words is large, all words can be decomposed into smaller units or elements (their building blocks). This is not the place to detail these units (syllables or letter sounds could stand as examples for the time being), the crucial point is that their number is relatively small. A writing system that depicts *these* units can, therefore, capitalize on this mental economy and provide the resource for representing an indefinitely large number of words.

This has not entirely discouraged, from time to time, attempts to produce a logographic system whose elements reflected units of meaning rather than sound. Up until the end of the sixteenth century Latin served as a *lingua franca* for the worlds of science, theology and letters. When, in the early 1600s, vernacular languages became more widely used the full impact of the curse bestowed on humanity by the builders of the Tower of Babel became apparent: scholars became cut off from one another by their different languages. At the same time, reports began to appear from China of a writing system that was understood by people with widely differing spoken languages. A number of attempts were made to produce a 'universal language' – an ideal writing system which would capture in a systematic way an exact classification of nature.

By far the most celebrated of such systems is that of John Wilkins, who was the first secretary to the Royal Society, and later Bishop of Chester. In 1668 he published his *Essay Towards a Real Character and a Philosophical Language*. This consisted of a revised English script containing thirty-seven characters which could be pronounced. These were applied to a classification scheme which attempted to categorize the natural world. To catch the flavour of Wilkins' scheme imagine the concept named by the word 'cat' can be systematically decomposed into a hierachy of basic elements (*an*imate, *non-hu*man, *quad*ruped, *dom*esticated, *fur*ry, etc.). If a character is assigned to each of these (for the sake of the example, say the letters italicized) then the 'word' *annonhuquaddomfur* takes on a peculiar status. To the reader who knows the meaning of the signs for these basic elements the 'word' yields up its sense in a way analogous to that found for pictographs. Obviously, if such an ideal writing system really worked it would be a major achievement for, regardless of their native language, all who read it would understand it. Further, since the scheme rests on an exact and logical classification of nature it would be an ideal medium for conveying scientific knowledge, admitting of no vagueness. Wilkins' book purported to demonstrate the practicality of his universal script (see Figure 1.9), but in fact neither it, nor any of its numerous rivals, has had any impact other than as whimsical curiosities. The reasons why such an attractive idea failed are instructive. In the first place there is bound to be an arbitrary element in any classification scheme. The science of the day – not nature – determines the distinctions that are drawn. Even the distinction between human and non-human can be seen on reflection to be less a property of nature than a complex cultural decision regarding the set of characteristics that define 'human'. In any case, not all features are easily described in terms of binary divisions: some are necessarily seen as triple, quadruple or multiple. Second, the hierarchical nature of such classification schemes is more than a little misleading. The levels in the hierarchy occupied by some attributes (that is, which dominate which) is uncertain in some cases. For example, why should 'domesticated' come before 'furry'? In other cases (see Figure 1.10) relationships may be implied that are not in fact a property of the real world at all, yet it seems impossible to remove them without arbitrarily distorting the representation. Finally, it has in any case proved impossible to arrive at any agreement as to what concepts are, in fact, properly seen as basic or primitive. The orderliness in nature which is implied by Bishop Wilkins' enterprise may be quite illusory. It is perhaps the case that our language is just about as economical, in this sense, as is necessary, and attempts to discover an underlying simplicity could be misguided. This is a subject to which we shall return, but for the moment it is enough to note that no ideal writing

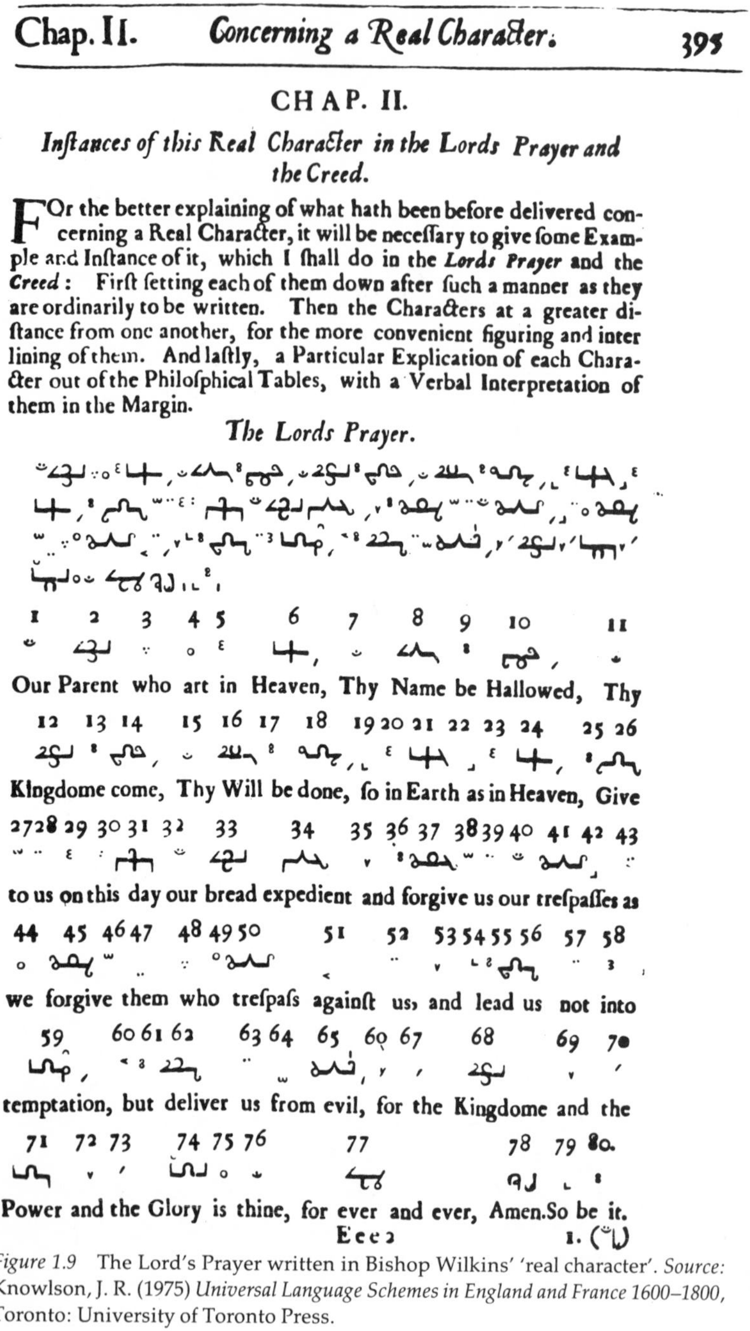

CHAP. II.

Inſtances of this Real Character in the Lords Prayer and the Creed.

FOr the better explaining of what hath been before delivered concerning a Real Character, it will be neceſſary to give ſome Example and Inſtance of it, which I ſhall do in the *Lords Prayer* and the *Creed* : Firſt ſetting each of them down after ſuch a manner as they are ordinarily to be written.   Then the Characters at a greater diſtance from one another, for the more convenient figuring and inter lining of them.   And laſtly, a Particular Explication of each Character out of the Philoſphical Tables, with a Verbal Interpretation of them in the Margin.

The Lords Prayer.

[real character symbols]

1   2   3   4 5   6   7   8   9   10   11

Our Parent who art in Heaven, Thy Name be Hallowed, Thy

12 13 14   15 16 17   18   19 20 21 22 23 24   25 26

Kingdome come, Thy Will be done, ſo in Earth as in Heaven, Give

27 28 29 30 31 32   33   34   35 36 37 38 39 40 41 42 43

to us on this day our bread expedient and forgive us our treſpaſſes as

44 45 46 47   48 49 50   51   52   53 54 55 56 57 58

we forgive them who treſpaſs againſt us, and lead us not into

59   60 61 62   63 64 65 66 67   68   69 70

temptation, but deliver us from evil, for the Kingdome and the

71 72 73   74 75 76   77   78 79 80.

Power and the Glory is thine, for ever and ever, Amen. So be it.

E e e 2   1.

Figure 1.9 The Lord's Prayer written in Bishop Wilkins' 'real character'. *Source:* Knowlson, J. R. (1975) *Universal Language Schemes in England and France 1600–1800,* Toronto: University of Toronto Press.

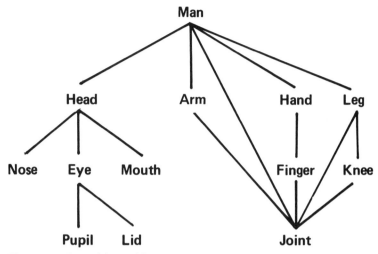

Figure 1.10   One of the problems in representing knowledge as a hierarchy of features is that contradictions occur. Here the feature 'joint' must be placed simultaneously at three 'levels'. *Source:* Kintsch, W. (1970) in D. A. Norman, *Models of Human Memory*, New York: Academic Press.

system of the kind suggested by Wilkins has ever been successfully devised.

The development of syllabaries

At least one major form of writing has remained at the stage of the phonographic representation of words. Chinese is a monosyllabic language that also makes use of changes in pitch to convey variations in meaning. Since the written form of Chinese does not signal what we would call 'letter sounds' a limited number of monosyllabic phonographs has to do duty for a vastly larger number of words. This is achieved by adding to the phonograph a particular distinguishing mark which suggests the sense in which it is used. For example, the single phonograph 'pa' began life as a pictographic representation of the tail of a mythical animal. As a phonograph it serves many different words: followed by a character for 'plant' it denotes a banana tree; with the sign for 'iron' it denotes a war chariot; with the sign for 'sickness' a scar. Although this writing system (see

PICTOGRAMS							
MAN, ANIMALS, AND PARTS OF THE HUMAN BODY							
MAN	WOMAN	CHILD	MOUTH	NOSE	EYE	HAND	FOOT
HORSE	TIGER	DOG	ELEPHANT	DEER	SHEEP	SILKWORM	TORTOISE
NATURAL AND ARTIFICIAL OBJECTS							
SUN	MOON	RAIN	LIGHTNING	MOUNTAIN	RIVER	GRAIN	WOOD
VASE	TRIPOD	BOW	ARROW	SILK	BOOK	ORACLE	OMEN

IDEOGRAMS			
FIGHTING (MAN AGAINST MAN)	PLOUGHING (MAN + PLOUGH)	HUNTING (WEAPON + ANIMAL)	SUCKLING (WOMAN NURSING CHILD)
SUNSET (SUN + GRASSES)	BRIGHT (MOON + WINDOW)	WRITING BRUSH (HAND + BRUSH)	SCRIBE (HAND + OBJECT)

ABOVE	BELOW

PICTOGRAM + PHONETIC ELEMENT			
BLACK HORSE (HORSE + li)	SACRIFICE (SPIRIT + ssu)	PREGNANCY (WOMAN + Jen)	HUAN RIVER (RIVER + huan)

HOMOPHONES	
(lai,'WHEAT,'FOR) lai 'TO COME'	(feng,'PHOENIX,'FOR) feng 'WIND'

Figure 1.11 Examples of Chinese pictograms and ideograms. Complex ideas (e.g. hunting) are depicted using combinations of pictograms (weapon plus animal). Pictograms may also be combined with characters representing sounds to produce novel meanings. The same sound (and ideogram) may represent two or more *different* meanings (homophones). *Source:* Diringer, D. (1977) *The Alphabet*, vol. 2, London: Hutchinson.

JAPANESE SYLLABARIES

PHONETIC VALUE	KATA KANA	HIRA GANA	PHONETIC VALUE	KATA KANA	HIRA GANA	PHONETIC VALUE	KATA KANA	HIRA GANA	PHONETIC VALUE	KATA KANA	HIRA GANA	PHONETIC VALUE	KATA KANA	HIRA GANA
i	イ	い	wa	ワ	わ	w(i)	ヰ	ゐ	sa	サ	さ			
ro	ロ	ろ	ka	カ	か	no	ノ	の	ki	キ	き			
fa (ha)	ハ	は	yo	ヨ	よ	o	オ	お	yu	ユ	ゆ			
ni	ニ	に	ta	タ	た	ku	ク	く	me	メ	め			
fo (ho)	ホ	ほ	re	レ	れ	ya	ヤ	や	mi	ミ	み			
fe (he)	ヘ	へ	so	ソ	そ	mä	マ	ま	si (shi)	シ	し			
to	ト	と	tu (tsu)	ツ	つ	ke	ケ	け	w(e)	ヱ	ゑ			
ti (chi)	チ	ち	ne	ネ	ね	fu	フ	ふ	fi (hi)	ヒ	ひ			
ri	リ	り	na	ナ	な	ko	コ	こ	mo	モ	も			
nu	ヌ	ぬ	ra	ラ	ら	e	エ	え	se	セ	せ			
ru	ル	る	mu	ム	む	te	テ	て	su	ス	す			
(w)o	ヲ	を	u	ウ	う	a	ア	あ	n	ン	ん			

Figure 1.12 Japanese KataKana and Hiragana syllabaries with their equivalent sounds. *Source:* Diringer, D. (1977) *The Alphabet*, vol. 2, London: Hutchinson.

a	e	i	o	u
a	e	i	o	u
ga	ge	gi	go	gu
ha	he	hi	ho	hu
la	le	li	lo	lu
ma	me	mi	mo	mu
na	ne	ni	no	nu
gwa	gwe	gwi	gwo	gwu
sa	se	si	so	su
da	de	di	do	du
dla	dle	dli	dlo	dlu
dza	dze	dzi	dzo	dzu
wa	we	wi	wo	wu
ya	ye	yi	yo	yu
ö	gö	hö	lö	nö
gwö	sö	dö	dlö	dzö
wö	yö	ka	hna	nah
s	ta	te	ti	tla

Figure 1.13 Modern American Indian syllabary using invented characters mixed with modified English letter forms. *Source:* Diringer, D. (1977) *The Alphabet*, vol. 2, London: Hutchinson.

Figure 1.11) maintains some of the advantages of direct representation (it is based on stylized pictographs) it has one serious weakness. To learn to read may involve very many years of study, possibly as long as twenty years to master the 40,000 or more words that can be written using the basic signs for a few hundred monosyllables.

Japanese is a polysyllabic language that makes use of signs derived from Chinese phonographs to signal syllable sounds. The technique of syllable representation (rather than whole word), however, proves to be enormously more efficient. With signs for only about fifty syllables all Japanese words can be written. In fact the Japanese syllabaries (see Figure 1.12), developed before the fourth century AD, are still in use. A considerably more recent creation is that of the syllabary for the North American Indian language, Cherokee. This syllabary, consisting of eighty-five signs (see Figure 1.13), was invented in 1821 by a native Indian called Sequoya. It is interesting to note that his first attempt at a written script for his language consisted of pictographs. Only when realizing how awkward this was did he devise the syllabary. Although Sequoya's script is no longer employed, it was in its time easily learned and effective.

There have been, of course, many other writing systems, but all appear to have progressed through the same developmental sequence: pictographic representation through rebus writing to some technique for representing sound.

The development of the alphabet

The ability to set down syllables rests, of course, on the linguistic insight that the sounds of single words are capable of being systematically and lawfully decomposed into smaller units: that is, that the word 'cactus' in English consists of two such units, one sounded as /cac/ and the other as /tus/. Both of these elements reappear in countless other words which have quite different meanings. From our modern perspective it may seem equally clear that syllables themselves are capable of further, regular decomposition into their component sounds. Once the fact is grasped that a very limited number of sounds can be disposed in various ways to form syllables, it is a small step to allocate unique written forms to the sounds. This step, however – the invention of the alphabet – was a very late development in historical terms. It is, in fact, a very considerable intellectual achievement. The reason for this relates to the rather peculiar status of the concept of 'letter' and the relationship that exists between sounds in a language and the means for displaying them. We shall discuss this issue in greater detail later, but it can be illustrated in general terms fairly readily.

The sound of a vowel – say the sound /a/ as in 'father' – could be said in some senses to be capable of an independent existence. This can be demonstrated simply by articulating it. The same is not the case for the /t/ in the word 'tap'. To articulate the sound /t/ always involves saying, in addition, some adjoining vowel: the 'pure' consonant cannot in the same sense exist alone. The invention of an alphabetic script with a symbol for the sound /a/, then, might be fairly straightforward since the event which the letter represents is readily accessible to users of the language; that is, the sound can be uttered in isolation. By contrast, the invention of a symbol for /t/ must follow from an appreciation of the fact that this *unpronounceable* sound is common to the words 'tap', 'tip', 'top', etc. in spite of the fact that attempts to utter this sound in each case will produce quite different results. In other words, the development of a fully alphabetic writing system involves a fundamental conceptual advance: the representation of consonants. Egyptian hieroglyphs can be shown to indicate a rudimentary alphabetic system to the extent that syllables were marked without a particular indication of the vowel to be employed (for example, the written forms 'ta' and 'tu' would not be distinguished). At an early stage in the development of written Egyptian an alphabetic method of representation appeared which, almost indifferently, allowed any of two or three signs to be used, not to convey their sense as pictographs, but to supply their initial sound. It was as if, in English, the signs for 'fir', 'flag' or 'five' could all be used equally well, not to portray the concept they were originally developed to represent, but to supply their initial sound /f/.

It was left to the Greeks to take the final step and make use of a writing system with signs to indicate vowel qualities. Once this has been done, of course, for a syllable such as 'ta' it follows quite naturally that the original sign for the syllable as a whole can be allowed to stand for the artificial concept of the consonant /t/.

The present alphabet of English and many other languages derives directly from Greek, but has at least some recognizable antecedents in Egyptian hieroglyphs. The power of a truly alphabetic writing system (Huey (1908) estimates no less than 250 to have been invented, of which about fifty survive) is that, with very limited resources (the repertoire of alphabetic signs), all the sounds necessary to characterize every word in a language may be represented. Some features of speech – for example, changes in pitch and rhythm – are admittedly rather poorly represented, if at all, but the point to be grasped is that an alphabetic writing system represents *speech*: speech itself acts as the primary vehicle for communication.

This introductory chapter has attempted to place the development of systems of writing alongside other techniques for representing thought. One powerful, indeed almost omniscient, method is the use of speech, but it is not the only one and the history of the development of writing shows a continual interplay between attempts to capture thought in the way that a painter might echo the reality of the visual world and attempts to represent speech itself. This latter enterprise, which forms the topic of much of this book, may be redefined as a continual growth in the understanding of language itself.

2
Making
sense
of
things

The visual and the conceptual world

In Chapter 1 a distinction was drawn between a visual world, in which objects could be said to define themselves in so far as their existence leads effortlessly to a conscious experience, and language, which was seen as one method (from among many) of representing aspects of mental life. This distinction can be made more explicit by an example. If a child asks of an object, 'What's that?', the conventional reply is one which accepts as common ground what the defining properties of the object are; that is, the adult unquestioningly accepts that the child is 'seeing' the same thing. The reply, 'That's a cow' will supply a name for this shared experience. Replies of the kind 'I see patches of black and white suspended in space' are, of course, accurate, but in the circumstances they are unnecessarily cautious. It is, after all, reasonable to assume that we all segment the visual world in more or less the same way. Contrast now the possible replies to the question 'What's a cow?'. This forces us into a *conceptual* world, divorced from the object present. We are, in a sense, asked to comment on properties of our language itself, the nuances of meaning. The common ground here – that which we may take as given in an interaction between two people – is much less obvious. Recall that the problem faced by ideal writing systems that attempt to mark orderly features of meaning is that such features are remarkably elusive. Definitions, as a few moments with any dictionary will reveal, are notoriously circular: they work because we are willing to refrain from asking awkward questions. Thus, if I am told that 'to kill' means 'cause to die', it is less than profitable to ask again what 'cause' means. While we are happy to believe that all people confronted by a cow see the same thing, it seems much less obvious that our thoughts can be fettered in the same way. What is lacking is an understanding of the units of thought. *Their* discovery has challenged scholars for centuries, and from time to time the unwelcome notion that they may be ultimately inaccessible has been advanced. Whichever way one looks at this, the practical fact remains that it is difficult to provide exact definitions within the symbolic domain that our language manipulates.

Physical features of speech

The problem of definition is of some significance when we consider the development of those writing systems that claim to be reflecting salient features of spoken language for it becomes necessary to ask what these features might be. Writing may well be characterized as a way of capturing attributes of speech in graphic form, but is this a sensible starting point? What *are* the defining characteristics of speech? Is it possible to know?

 The most obvious initial attack on this question is to ask what can be measured physically. Speech is, after all, a measurable acoustic event in the world. It is possible that we can interrogate this event in much the same way as child may by asking, 'What's that?'. One immediate problem presents itself, however. Speech is an event in time. In order to report on it we must either rely on memory (which, over long periods of time, is patently impractical) or devise some way of recording the acoustic event as faithfully as possible. However, such physical measurements are themselves representations, albeit we are often tempted to forget the fact. For the time being perhaps this objection can be ignored if by measuring speech we can discover which acoustic events signal differences in meaning.

If a speaker says two words – say 'cat' and 'pat' – it is possible to measure such physical features as changes in amplitude and frequency and timing of the sound waves. At first sight it might seem that to isolate the defining features of speech it should be only necessary to measure such physical changes and see how they correspond to decisions as to which word was heard. There are some immediate snags here, however. We were possibly unwise to ignore the fact that the physical measurements made led to *representations* of the event, they were not the event itself. Coming to the problem without any preconceptions we have no idea at all at what physical level we should be recording possible differences. Are these to be found in the coarse grain of the sound; that is, in events changing over seconds? Or are the critical events only to be disovered in the microstructure of changes occurring in thousandths (or millionths) of seconds? Obviously we can make some guesses from knowing something about the way speech is produced. (For instance, there is a limit on the rate at which the vocal chords can vibrate.) This serves to place some constraint on the collection of physical data, but the scope of possible variation in the data we collect still remains indefinitely large. There is a paradox here: having collected all the data, we may be fairly certain that we have captured the 'essential' difference, yet still not know what or where it is, as if, having lost a ring on the seashore, we 'find' it by scooping up all the sand on the beach. Except, of course, the analogy here is a weak one, since if we search for a hidden object we at least know what we are looking for, and thus have ways of knowing when it has been found. Unfortunately, this condition is not met in the search for the physical characteristics that distinguish 'cat' from 'pat'. The point being made is that the decision to make physical measurements is always bound up with some other *theoretical* decision as to what to record: as Alan Newell put it, in a memorable phrase, you can't play Twenty Questions with nature and expect to win. If this line of argument appears unnecessarily abstract or farfetched then it is easy to illustrate the difficulty in concrete terms.

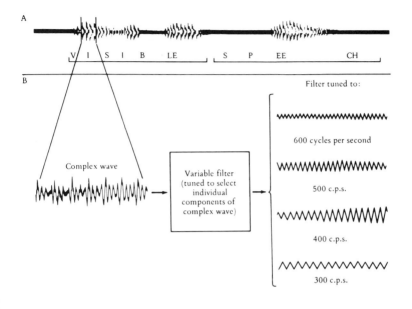

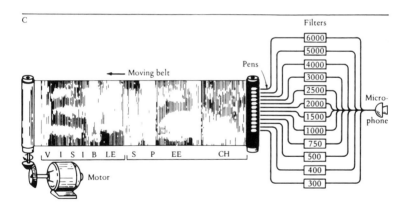

Figure 2.1 The speech spectrogram. 'A' shows an oscillograph tracing. 'B' illustrates how sounds of different frequency can be selected (by means of filters) from a complex sound. 'C' shows in schematic form the preparation of a spectrographic record of the words 'visible speech'. Time is represented by the movement of the paper band. Sounds of varying frequency are presented through filters. Intensity is shown by the darkness of the pen recording. From Potter, R. K., Kopp, G. A. and Kopp, H. G. (1966) *Visual Speech*, Murray Hill, N.J.: Bell Telephone Laboratories, Inc.

The physical properties that can most readily be extracted from an audible signal are changes over time in pitch and loudness. Although there are several possible ways of representing these dimensions, it is customary to produce a graph with pitch on the Y axis and time on the X axis. The volume of the sound (that is, the amount of energy it contains) may then be portrayed by variations in the darkness of the marks which signal a sound of a particular pitch at a particular time. This mode of representation is known as a speech spectogram (see Figure 2.1). In effect, although there is some energy present at all frequencies, speech is characterized by a number of dark horizontal bands (known as formants). These occur, over time, simultaneously at a number of different frequencies. The two words 'cat' and 'pat', spoken by the same person, are set out in this way in Figure 2.2. Obviously, there are differences between these figures, but it is hard to know which is significant. Figure 2.2 also shows spectograms of the word 'cat' spoken by another person. The problem now is more severe: it is very difficult indeed to isolate which of the innumerable differences relate to differences between people and which to differences between words. Indeed, the crucial differentiating marks are simply not evident at all. Were they to be so, of course, the records in Figure 2.2 would comprise a form of writing: in fact an ideal form, namely *visible speech*. It is the case that a few individuals, after a lot of practice, can learn to decode such records. However, this is far from saying that the records declare their referents in the way that objects in the visual world do. There is no reason why they should, of course, since they are *not* objects in the visual world, but representations of auditory events. To identify the salient features of speech from such a record we must have some idea of what we are looking for; that is, we must have some concept of the nature of language. All normal human beings understand speech (presented in an auditory mode, that is). The human nervous system has evolved to identify its salient or defining features. This is not to say that we can become aware of what these elements are simply by taking thought or using intuition. In the visual modality drawings serve as good representations of objects. We might guess, therefore, that, for speech, an equally effective representation would have to be presented in the auditory modality. And

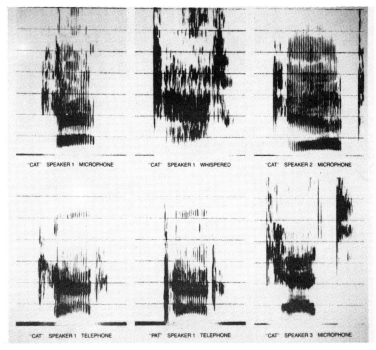

Figure 2.2 Speech spectrograms of the words 'cat' and 'pat' spoken in different circumstances and by different speakers. *Source:* Lehiste, I. (ed.) (1967) *Readings in Acoustic Phonetics*, Cambridge, Mass.: M.I.T. Press.

indeed, such 'shorthand' speech has been produced – taking the form of highly schematic spectograms which, when converted back to sound, produce recognizable speech (see Figure 2.3).

Psychological features of speech

If we cannot define speech easily in acoustic terms, is it possible to isolate the psychologically relevant variables? In other words, what information does the hearer actually use when speech is decoded? Which of the innumerable acoustic variations we have identified are actually significant, and which are not? This last is a question that has been examined by linguists for many centuries and it is possible to give both a general answer in terms

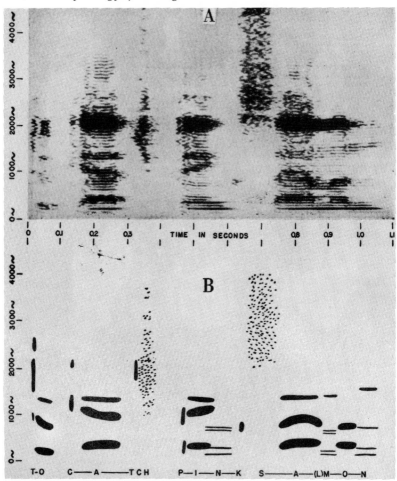

Figure 2.3 Speech spectrogram of the phrase 'to catch pink salmon'. The lower part of the figure shows a schematic spectrogram derived from the original, which when reproduced as sound is recognizable. *Source:* Lehiste, I. (ed.) (1967) *Readings in Acoustic Phonetics*, Cambridge, Mass.: M.I.T. Press.

of some of the principles involved, and also go some way towards giving specific answers for a particular language such as English. The general principles can be simply grasped by looking at Figure 2.4 representing an (idealized) sound spectrogram of the word 'bag' spoken in isolation. Both in terms of its written form (the letters 'b', 'a' and 'g') and in terms of intuitions about its acoustic 'constituent elements' (the sounds /b/, /a/, /g/) one arrives at a belief that there are three identifiable elements in the spoken and written form of this word. This is as it should be if the written forms signal speech as distinct from signalling something about the object itself through a pictogram (i.e. a picture of a bag). The written sequence of letters appears to

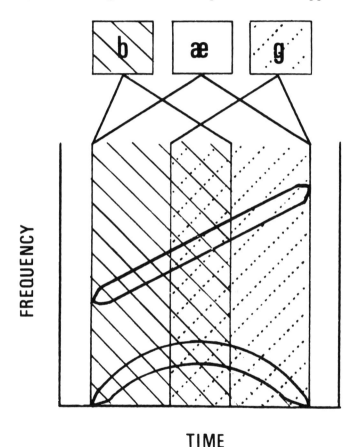

TIME

Figure 2.4 Schematic speech spectrogram of the word 'bag'. It is clear that the vowel sound is continuous, there are no discrete elements relating to the individual letters. The influence of the acoustic events relating to each letter overlap in time.

refer to something other than three distinct *acoustic* events: it relates to what might be termed three *psychologically* significant distinctions. The term 'phone' is used to refer to these distinctions in speech sounds which allow words in a language to be distinguished. The significant psychological question is *how* the hearer moves from an analysis of the speech signal to arrive at a categorization in terms of phones.

We have already seen the difficulties which arise if we suggest that there exist in the speech signal particular acoustic events that uniquely signal particular phones in a one-to-one fashion. If such a simple relationship existed it would have many important implications, since it would allow for the construction of machines capable of detecting phonetic variation which could then respond appropriately to natural speech. As we know, progress in this direction has been very slow for several reasons. The first and most obvious difficulty such a hypothetical 'phone detector' must face relates to the fact that the signals associated with a particular phone cannot be absolute. To demonstrate this, consider the fact that phonetic discrimination is accomplished with equal ease whether we listen to a child or to an adult, or indeed whether we listen to the voices of men or women. This, despite the fact that the *absolute* average pitch of these different sources varies by hundreds of cycles per second. Any mechanism, therefore, which can detect phonetic variation must deal with *relative* values. Whatever the acoustic clues are, they cannot be defined in terms of a particular distribution of physical energy; but the problem by no means ends here. We can observe in Figure 2.4 that the acoustic signal itself varies *continuously* across the duration of a spoken word, yet our perception – or at least our intuitions – about words is that they are comprised of discrete elements. As may be seen, the vowel in 'bag' casts its influence over both the initial and final consonants. Its effects may be seen to spread across the whole word. How, then, can one sensibly ask where in the signal the sound /a/ begins and ends? In speaking, the articulators are in a continual state of change, moving smoothly from one position to another. Thus, the vowel sound in 'pot' and 'sog' is in fact signalled by quite distinct acoustic events, since the movements of the vocal apparatus producing it start in different positions as a result of the different initial consonants, and end in different final positions. The method we employ for detecting phonetic variation must, therefore, be sensitive to context. The same acoustic event will, in different contexts, signal different phones. Similarly, different acoustic signals may come to be classified (i.e. heard) as the same phonetic event.

This somewhat bewildering assertion can, in fact, be demonstrated quite simply by means of a psychological experiment. In 1957 Ladefoged and Broadbent made use of an artificially produced sound which was carefully recorded in two different contexts. Presented in isolation, the sound produced the effect of someone saying the word 'bet'. The two different contexts used were either a voice with an overall high pitch saying, 'Please say what this word is', or the same phrase said in a low-pitched voice. The results were quite striking. Subjects presented with the first tape frequently reported hearing the word 'bit'. Subjects in the second condition frequently reported hearing 'bat'. In both cases the judgements were made with confidence. Phone detection seems to involve making inferences about characteristics of the person producing the sounds. In this context the word 'inference' is used merely as a way of describing behaviour, it is not intended to imply a conscious process.

Perceptual categories

There is, however, one final observation which, more than any other, makes the notion of a simple acoustic definition of phones probably invalid. This is the *discontinuous* nature of human phone detection. The effects here are readily demonstrated, though they are rather more difficult to describe. Imagine the word 'slit' recorded on tape. If a very brief period of silence of gradually increasing length is inserted electronically into the word the perception of what we hear changes from 'slit' to 'split'. The important point is, however, that this perceived change is *abrupt*: we do not have the impression of one word gradually blending to another. Our perception is that the word is either one thing or another, there is no middle ground where it is heard as a little like both (see Figure 2.5). If we choose to define phones in terms of bundles of particular sounds we would not expect this

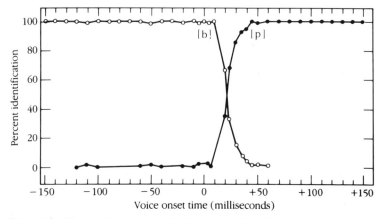

Figure 2.5   The time between parting the lips and starting to sound is referred to as voice onset time. This can be varied gradually. The figure shows the percentage of judgements as to whether what is heard is a 'p' or a 'b'. Note that the decision changes abruptly at about 25 msec. Thus, a continuous change in the signal produces a discontinuous categorical change in perception. *Source:* Lisker and Abramson (1970).

result. Perception should vary continuously. The fact that perception varies in a discontinuous fashion means that our chosen definition is unsatisfactory. This particular cognitive problem appears to be solved in a different way.

The starting point for a more satisfactory view is to consider again the question of how we identify some familiar object in the real world, such as a chair. Is this achieved by making use of a pre-defined set of features such as arms, legs, back, etc? The answer must be no, since, whatever set of features we choose, widely different visual events (that is, things other than chairs) may satisfy particular feature tests. Worse than this, the features themselves will have to be very vague (e.g. that a chair 'is something to sit on'). Definitions for such notions are not readily available since they draw on a wide range of knowledge. To see an object as a chair involves a decision, albeit an unconscious one, *not* to see it simultaneously as something else. Visual perception is certainly categorial. We do not experience objects, for example, that are some way between, say, a chair and something else. Similarly, when we observe ambiguous line drawings such as those in Figure 2.6 we see either one figure or

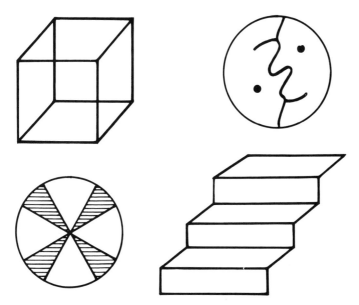

Figure 2.6 Ambiguous figures. Our perception of what these drawings represent undergoes a continual alternation between two states.

another, we do not see both versions at the same time. The data here don't change, but the decision does.

The case is that there exist mental events – we may call them ideas – that represent our knowledge of, among other things, objects in the real world. Physical events (sights and sounds) serve to activate this knowledge. Our perception – that is, our conscious experience of seeing, hearing or touching something – is the activation of this knowledge. The currency (the stimulus event itself) in this exchange seems always to purchase more than it is worth. Physical stimuli in all modalities are often incomplete and contaminated by other, irrelevant information; yet our perceived world is in general very stable. It is so because of what we know: a large number of different patterns of stimulus information (the input) serve to evoke a single conceptual decision (the output).

The isolation of phones is achieved in just this way: no single acoustic event acts as sufficient evidence to produce the idea of a particular phone; rather, there is a whole range of events, any or all of which can be taken as possible sources of evidence. Thus, phones are perceptual events (one might say *mental* events), but this is not to deny them a stable existence, they exist alongside other perceived events in the real world as the result of an interaction between physical stimulation and knowledge. The continuously varying speech signal is, by this process, effectively cut up into a limited set of distinct units. These are the 'sounds' that are available to convey differences in meaning in a language. These sounds, in fact, relate to the particular discriminations that the auditory system in the human brain can make. All languages use the same set, but none uses all possible discriminable sounds. To discuss the phonetic discriminations made in a particular language it is useful to employ another term: the *phoneme*. The difference between phones and phonemes is· exactly that which introduced this chapter: one relates to the common ground of perceptions, the other to the more shadowy region of shared ideas. The phoneme is the name for a particular classification, it is a conceptual matter. Concepts – for example, our notion of what is needed for an object to be classed as a chair – cannot be tied in a one-to-one fashion to events in the physical world. (You need only settle on an upturned log to eat a picnic lunch to appreciate this point.) It is this set of concepts – ideas about sounds – that is represented by an alphabetic script.

Alphabetic writing systems signal phonemes. That is, they mark the set of sound differences that our language employs to signal changes in meaning. We have a writing system that indicates to the reader, not particular sounds but, rather, particular sets of sounds which in our language are treated as equivalent. What we have not as yet considered is the extent to which the phonetic discriminations we have described are learned.

The biological endowment

Since different phones are employed in different languages it is clear that at least some of the conceptual knowledge is learned through early language experience. There are, however, properties of the brain that set limits on the kind of sensory discriminations that can be made. There is good evidence that human beings possess brain tissue that is biologically adapted for the processing of speech. For example, very young infants appear to respond to speech-like sounds in a categorial way. That is, while the speech cue varies continuously the baby's response shows a marked change at phonetic boundaries. In fact, the evidence suggests that the infant at first possesses a wide range of in-built categories and these are in some way 'tuned' by the speech environment. One powerful reflection of this fact is the ability of young children to acquire *any* natural language. Within a few years this plasticity has vanished and by adulthood it is (sadly) virtually impossible to master a new language, in the sense of being able to speak it with a native accent. One's existing phonetic repertoire has to make do. All children, then, possess what might be termed 'discovery procedures' (specialized, pre-existing brain functions) designed to isolate and identify the properties of the particular language or languages to which they may be exposed. It should be emphasized that this is to claim no more for language than might be claimed for perception in general. 'Regularities' in the world do not simply impose themselves on us. The nature of the observer (that is, the structure and organization of the receptive mechanisms) sets limits on, and in part predetermines, what may or may not be perceived.

In summary, it is suggested that acoustic events (properties of the physical world) capture particular conceptual representations by a process that involves, among other things, drawing (unconscious) inferences about properties of the device which produced the sound. Articulation is a kind of gesture; understanding speech involves modelling the gesture.

Categories of writing

The implications of all this for reading and writing may now be made a little clearer. Alphabetic writing systems are methods of casting the significant distinctions of speech (phonemes) into a graphic form. They do not attempt to record all possible distinctions, but merely to provide enough information to allow the reader to arrive at meaning. The categorization of letters in an alphabetic writing system presents a perceptual task identical in most aspects to the categorization of phones. For example, there does not exist in the real world a single, 'legal' representation of the letter 'a': all the forms shown in Figure 2.7 are acceptable examples. Obviously, there is no limit to the number of variations that could be produced. The reason for this is that the notion of an 'a' is not an event in the real world at all, but part

Figure 2.7   Various representations of the letter 'a'.

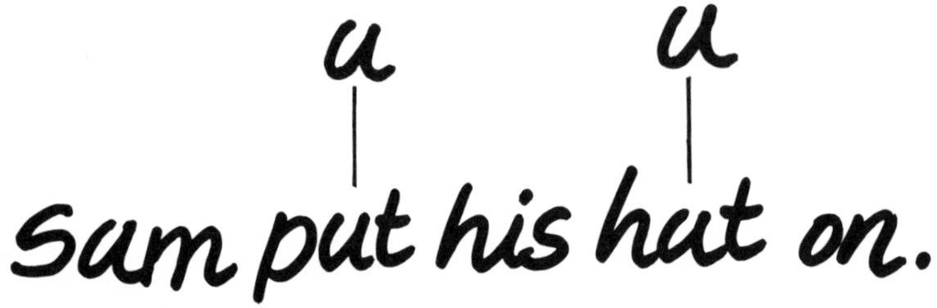

Figure 2.8   The two forms in the upper part of the figure are not acceptable examples of letters if presented out of context. They are, however, acceptable in the handwritten sentence shown below.

of our conceptual knowledge; it is an idea. Further, it is an idea that leans on other related ideas about the significant phonemic distinctions in our language. This is not to argue that at some boundary condition a signal may fail. The forms in the upper part of Figure 2.8 are *not* acceptable examples of the letter 'a'. They may be acceptable, however, if the reader is allowed to bring a broader knowledge to bear on this interpretation, as when they are inserted into the words shown in Figure 2.8.

Knowledge and perception

We have now considered both physical and psychological characteristics in our attempt to arrive at the defining features of language. There is a third and final level of analysis. This takes into account the *interaction* between conceptual knowledge and perception; that is, the fact that the relationship between physical event and mental category is not all one-way: the system of ideas itself determines the manner in which physical data are processed. Conscious experience quite often involves what we might term guesswork, either because there is not enough stimulus information present (the identification of letters in Figure 2.8 is an example of this) or because we are unwilling or unable to make use of what evidence we have. If we look at a solid object, such as a chair, we are usually willing to believe it to be so even when we cannot see all round it or touch it. In fact, of course, the world is not full of the sort of tricks illustrated in Figure 2.9, and our judgements are usually safe in this respect. It is easy to become confused about what is going on when an observer examines some vague or fragmentary stimulus

Figure 2.9 Drawings of objects seen from an unusual point of view. The difficulty we experience recognizing these suggests that some internal representations of objects are better than others.

Figure 2.10   The spotted dog. Although the dog is hard to spot, once identified, clear contours around its form become visible. *Source:* Ronald James, photographer.

like that in Figure 2.10 and decides that it is an instance of some particular category. Obviously, the decision itself *adds* nothing to the stimulus information. It should rather be seen as being based on evidence that may, in extreme cases, be at the limit of what can be taken as a 'safe bet'. Normally such processes flow along well enough and unregarded. There are, though, enough instances where the perceptual decisions taken prove to be wrong for us to catch a glimpse of the system in action. The train we sit in may seem to pull out only for us to discover that it was the train opposite that moved. The person we recognize across the street may turn out not to be the friend we supposed. In spite of countless re-readings printed errors go undetected. All these illustrations exemplify the interaction between an observer's knowledge of the world and the processing of particular stimulus information. The interaction reveals processes that are both selective and constructive. A certain conceptual decision serves to direct attention selectively towards one feature in the physical world rather than towards another. Sometimes we pay a price for this by losing information from elsewhere. Normal skilled readers, for example, do not look at each word of what they read, yet their understanding may be unimpaired. This is particularly evident when the material in question is very familiar. In this case, reading can take the form of a cursory skimming and the substantial increase in reading speed can be seen as simply a function of the fact that the physical information available (in this case particular sequences of letters) invariably confirms a particular set of conceptual decisions.

In all circumstances the perceived world (including the world of words and letters) is based on selective sampling from among available stimuli. The continuity, stability and homogeneity of our conscious experience is underpinned by a complex set of conceptual decisions which are driven by an input mechanism that is sampling the environment selectively. A reader's general conceptual knowledge also operates to facilitate the processes of constructive perception. Again, this is not to argue that something is *added* to the stimulus itself, but that its interpretation relies on knowledge not necessarily triggered directly by the stimulus. Much of what we read is written on the assumption that powerful strategies of this kind can be readily deployed. To read fluently means to draw valid inferences from what is written, and these inferences permit the reader to go well beyond what is explicitly stated.

3
Language games

The language of thought

It will probably have become apparent from the first two chapters of this book that grappling with the problems of reading and writing involves understanding ideas drawn from both psychology and linguistics. For this reason, the first section of this chapter tries to set out in some detail the relationship between these two disciplines.

Everyone who knows a language possesses certain skills. These include the power to produce and understand sentences, and the ability to decide whether or not a sentence is grammatical. It is rather difficult, however, to say exactly what is meant by the assertion that a person knows a language. How can this knowledge be described? A complete inventory will not be possible, since the number of sentences we can produce and understand is effectively infinite. We all meet entirely new ones every day. One possible solution is provided by the discipline of linguistics. This is to describe a set of rules that, when applied, could produce grammatical sentences. The rules themselves make no direct reference to the *content* of sentences. They deal with their structure, making use of such abstract notions as 'noun', 'noun-phrase', 'subject', 'verb' and so on. A perfect set of rules would provide the linguist with the means for describing, in abstract terms, all possible sentences in a particular language. Further, the rules would proscribe all sentences that a native speaker would find ungrammatical. Thus, the rule system would provide a place for sentences such as

John was beating his head on the wall.

or

while sitting, Louise let her thoughts wander.

or any number of other 'grammatical' sentences. At the same time, the rules would be violated by sentences such as

John was beating his idea on the wall.

or

while ought, Louise let her thoughts wander.

A complete set of such rules is a *grammar* of the language. In one sense this provides an answer to the question of what the speaker knows: it is the grammar. However, this can prove to be a rather unmanageable idea. It is well enough to claim someone knows a grammar, but does this not, in fact, simply push the problem back a step? What does it mean when we say someone knows a set of rules? If we analyse the statement we find it is ambiguous. It could mean (1) the person uses the rules to do certain things. In which case it would be sensible to ask if the person was aware of this. Possibly, in the right circumstances, the person could actually tell us what the rules were. Alternatively, it could mean no more than (2) a claim that some observer (a linguist, for example) could, by inventing a set of rules, make sense of the person's speech. This second claim is much more modest. It involves claiming neither that the person uses the rules nor even is aware of them – it simply asserts that the person *follows* them.

Lest this appear too paradoxical, consider an illustrative example. Imagine a man playing cricket. We can say, as spectators, that he knows how to play the game; that is, as a batsman, he may in the right circumstances play a cover drive or a hook shot. He will not, for example, try to catch the ball in his hands. Each example of a particular shot will be slightly different. We could claim that he is capable of producing an indefinitely large number of them. If we wish to say what this person *knows* we can, as a shorthand, say he knows the rules of the game. In other words, he knows which strokes are 'permissible'. However, it should be made explicit that this *is* merely a shorthand expression. We do not want to claim that, in making a stroke, the player actually *employs* the rules of cricket in the sense of using them in sequence like a cook using a recipe book. Rather, the rules are a way of making sense of the player's performance. Borrowing the terms used in Chapter 2 we can say that a variety of different evidence can be used to gain access to a particular concept. Thus we, as observers, declare that a shot was a 'cover drive' or a 'hook'.

In the case of the language user, the grammar provides a similar way of imposing order on a set of observations. However, there are many ways of doing this (that is, there are many possible grammars), and we must not fall into the error of treating the rule system as equivalent to a set of psychological processes. The speaker does not consult the rule book any more than the batsman does. A grammar is simply a description of a language. Whether it is a good grammar or not relates to how effectively it can be used to categorize the sentences of a language. It is different in this respect from a scientific theory that a psychologist may propose to explain how a person speaks and understands speech. The grammar's validity is tested ultimately against the intuitions of native speakers (i.e. what they claim to know). In contrast, a psychological theory is a statement about actual mental processes. This can only be tested by experimentation.

To summarize, a grammar is a rule system which an observer can use to classify utterances. As such, it relates most directly to the conceptual categories of the observer. There are as many possible grammars as human ingenuity may devise; that is, their number is unlimited. Yet it would be a scandal to make a similar claim about a psychological theory. That should refer to actual processes – not what *might* go on, but what *really does* go on in the human mind. Thus, of all the myriad grammars, we would like to believe that one alone will describe not only the observer's categories but also the mental states of the speaker. Such a grammar would obviously be of special interest to psychologists. However, at present, we are far from knowing what it is. We do not have a 'psychological process grammar'. For the time being, linguistics and psychology must live in related, but different, conceptual worlds.

The language of vision

In Chapter 2 it was suggested that the way the brain is constructed (for example, the organization of the visual system) may play a part in determining which properties of the world we come to accept as defining features of objects. In one sense this is obvious. If we were equipped to detect infra-red light directly objects would take on visual properties related to their temperatures. We would then see a different set of things from those we see at present. In another sense the implications of the proposition are far less obvious. To explore this further we need to consider which aspects of the perceived world arise from the way the brain is constructed and which result from processes of experience and learning.

We could characterize the process of growing up and adapting to the environment as a process of discovery. In particular, the child must discover, in a continually changing world of sights and sounds, which properties do not change. Consider the countless different shapes a moving object will convey to the eye, yet it comes to be seen as a single 'thing'. A variety of different evidence comes to evoke a particular idea. It is worthwhile taking time over this proposition, since it leads to consequences that run counter to our usual intuitions about the way the world works. What is being argued is that for the psychologist the division between the physical world of *things* and the mental world of *ideas* is not particularly helpful. One consequence of this has already been developed. This is that stimulus information comes to be categorized in one way rather than another as a consequence of our experience, or simply because we are built that way. There is a second aspect to the argument. The manner in which we see the world is constrained by the ideas we hold about it. To accept this is to abandon the common sense view that the natural world simply *is* the way it is, and that it imposes its structure on us. For evidence we must look at the way ideas about the world determine how it is seen.

'Theory-driven' observation

The history of science yields many examples of the influence that theories about an object have over the way it is seen. Some of the most straightforward are found in anatomical observation. Common sense would suggest that the structure of human organs should be apparent enough to the observer who, if skilful enough, should be able to portray them accurately. Early observations on the structure of the human heart certainly serve to cast doubt on this view. To illustrate the point a brief digression is called for. One of the earliest systematic discussions of the function of the heart was put forward by Aristotle (384–322 BC). His idea was that the heart had three chambers, a left, a right and a central 'common' chamber. His early statements on the nature of blood suggested that impure, thick blood sank to the lower parts and pure, fine blood rose to the head. Galen (150–200 AD), the most celebrated founding father of medicine, took over some of Aristotle's ideas but was scornful of the idea of a three-chambered heart. He could not understand how Aristotle could ever have seen it in this way. Galen's view of the heart is shown in Figure 3.1(a). The details need not concern us. What is important is his view of the heart as having *two* chambers and the notion that the septum which divided these was, to a degree, permeable. Galen claimed there were minute channels which allowed one side to communicate with the other. He did not know, of course, about the heart's action as a pump. This was not understood until Harvey's observations were published in 1628 (see Figure 3.1(b)). Now there is little doubt (in spite of periods of opposition from the Church) that human dissection under scientific conditions took place frequently in the time between Galen and Harvey. The question to be

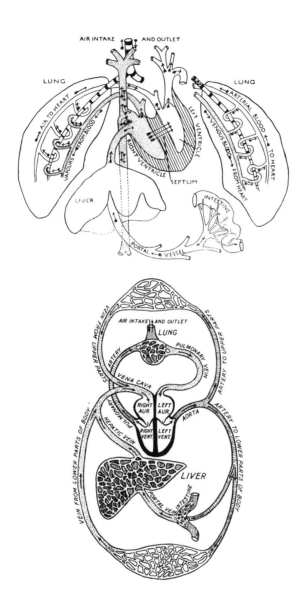

Figure 3.1(a) (top)   Diagram of the heart and blood vessels according to Galen (AD 150–200). Note the two-chambered heart with the tiny passages between the dividing tissue clearly indicated. *Source:* Singer, C. (1925) *The Evolution of Anatomy*, London: Kegan Paul.

(b) (bottom)   The circulation of the blood according to the theory put forward by William Harvey in 1628. *Source:* Singer, C. (1956) *The Discovery of the Circulation of the Blood*, Folkestone: Dawson & Sons Ltd.

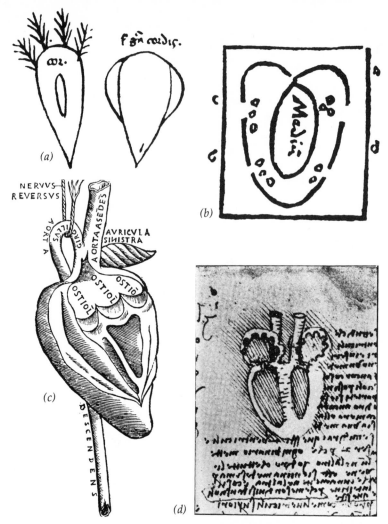

Figure 3.2(a) The heart as shown in the Roncioni manuscript, Pisa, first half of thirteenth century. *Source:* Singer, C. (1921) *Studies in the History and Method of Science*, Oxford: Oxford University Press.

(b) The heart, drawn by Johannes Adelphus (1513). Note the two ventricles, plus a 'common' ventricle. *Source:* Singer, C. (1925) *The Evolution of Anatomy*, London: Kegan Paul.

(c) The heart, drawn by Besengar (1532). Note the shape of the valves and the auricle shown as being 'chochlear' (whence, 'the Cockles of the Heart'). *Source:* Singer, C. and Rubin, C. (1946) *A Prelude to Modern Science*, Cambridge: Cambridge University Press.

(d) The heart, drawn by Leonardo (1452–1519), in the early sixteenth century. Note the passages and the two chambers. *Source:* Singer, C. (1921) *Studies in the History and Method of Science*, Oxford: Oxford University Press.

Figure 3.3   Self-portrait by Leonardo (1452–1519).

answered, therefore, is why, in this case, was the heart not seen to be as it is? The figures in Figure 3.2 were all made from observation. In Figures 3.2(a) and 3.2(b) an Aristotelian three-chambered heart was observed. In Figure 3.2(c) what we know as valves were completely misdrawn. Could it be simply that these observations were the product of unskilled surgeons and poor or careless draughtsmen? Figure 3.2(d) suggests not: this was a sketch (one of several) made by Leonardo after a careful dissection. The shape is peculiar (though not as much as some of the earlier drawings), but most revealing is the clear indication of the links (postulated by Galen) between the two chambers. It can hardly be asserted that Leonardo could not draw what lay before him (see Figure 3.3); rather, the conclusion appears forced that until the *function* of the heart was understood it was not 'seen' correctly. Theories about the nature of the world appear to play a considerable role in the process of observation. A drawing – even a very detailed one – must be looked on as some kind of theory about the structure of the world. It is probably for this reason that to this day textbooks of physiology employ drawings rather than photographs.

In Figure 3.4 a similar catalogue of misperception can be seen. In this case drawings of sections of the eye consistently mislocate the lens. Figures 3.4(a) and (b) were drawn from observation by Leonardo and reflect the view that vision involves the eye (the crystalline sphere) radiating outwards. The idealized mathematical conception of the eye by Roger Bacon (Figure 3.4(c)) perpetuates the error, as does the drawing by Vesalius. It is important to appreciate that these illustrations are not works of the imagination, such as Dürer's famous 'armoured' rhinoceros (see Figure 3.5(a) to be compared with what was probably a drawing from nature in Figure 3.5(b)). Neither are these the mere inventions of a credulous age, such as Topsell's drawing of the Lamia (Figure 3.5(c)), which was 'known' to exist (like the unicorn) because of its presence in the Bible (as Lilith). They stand in complete contrast, as careful, on-the-spot records. Yet it appears inevitable that between the object and the representation thought must intervene, and this cognitive activity will determine what is seen. As a final, and strangely touching, example consider the very first observations by microscope.

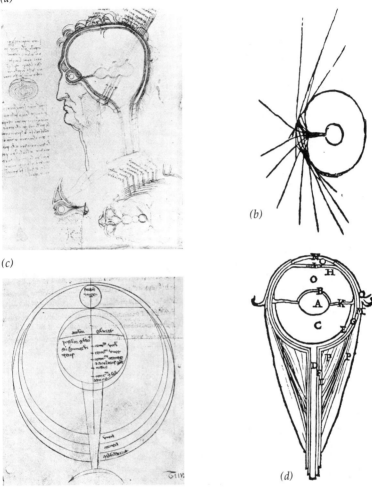

Figure 3.4(a and b) Drawings in section of the human eye made by Leonardo (1452–1519). Note that the lens is placed centrally – as the 'seat of vision'. *Source:* (a) Singer, C. (1921) *Studies in the History and Method of Science*, Oxford: Oxford University Press, and (b) Singer, C. (1925) *The Evolution of Anatomy*, London: Kegan Paul.

(c) Diagram of the eye from a thirteenth-century manuscript by Roger Bacon. Note that the various layers are shown to lie in exact mathematical proportion to each other. The lens is shown at the centre. *Source:* Singer, C. (1925) *The Evolution of Anatomy*, London: Kegan Paul.

(d) The eye, drawn by Vesalius (1543). Again, note the position of the lens – marked by the letter 'A'. *Source:* Singer, C. (1925) *The Evolution of Anatomy*, London: Kegan Paul.

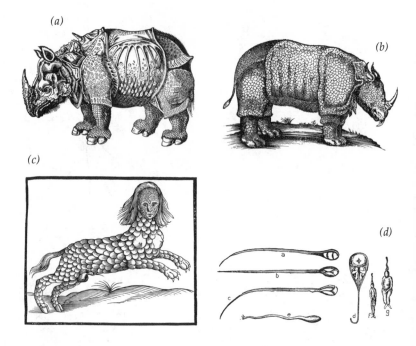

Figure 3.5(a) Drawing of rhinoceros by Albrecht Dürer (1515). *Source:* Topsell, E. (1607) *The Historie of Four-footed Beastes,* London.

(b) Rhinoceros as drawn in Jacob Bondt's (1658) *Historiae naturalis & medicae Indiae orientalis,* Amsterdam.

(c) Drawing of 'the true picture of the Lamia'. *Source:* Topsell, E. (1607) *The Historie of Four-footed Beastes*, London.

(d) Early observations of spermatozoa under the microscope. By Leeuwenhoek (1679), Hartsocker (1694) and Plantades (1699). *Source:* Singer, C. (1959) *A Short History of Scientific Ideas*, Oxford: Oxford University Press.

Figure 3.5(d) shows drawings made from observations of human spermatazoa. In this case, theories about the origin of life cast a powerful influence over what was seen.

Constructive perception

The point of view represented by all these illustrations is often referred to by psychologists as 'constructive' perception, but the term is possibly unfortunate. It suggests active, conscious processes of organization on the part of the perceiver, whereas the theoretical inferences which lead to distortions in representation or to a particular view of the world may occur quite unconsciously. In any case, the nervous system itself imposes a degree of structure on the perceived world, and it is clearly peculiar to refer to the processes in that case (that is, within the 'hardware' of the brain) as 'inferences' at all.

Human beings appear to operate in their environment with two kinds of process. The first flows from the intrinsic organization of the nervous system. The brain is a device which possesses certain theories about the world before it is ever confronted with actual sense data. This is not quite such a wild claim as may first appear. It is to argue that the processes of natural selection have endowed us with potential to make some perceptual distinctions and not others. The second process flows from the nature of thought itself. We lay claim to theories about our world. We understand how things work. This knowledge is hard-won, yet once achieved can be communicated with relative ease to others. Our power to symbolize in this way is certainly what sets us apart from other possibly sentient beings. Our development is in part a process of learning to perceive. That is, there is an interaction between a nervous system that has evolved exquisite skills for extracting, for example, features of the visual world, and the mind. The function of mind is to develop and elaborate theories about the organization and function of properties of the world. This ability to construct a mental model of the world endows huge biological advantages since it converts an organism that merely *responds* into one that *acts*; that is, the model of the world we hold (which will be a shorthand expression of its salient features) allows us to predict the outcomes of our potential actions in great detail.

Thus the term 'perceptual learning' is not at all the contradiction it first appears. It refers to the development of an ability to resolve distinctions with increasing specificity in the perceived world. In concrete terms being able to differentiate between stimulus events means being able to *see* them as different: that is, the ability to assign a unique response to an increasing number of distinct events. A 'real' world does indeed thrust itself upon the perceiver – it is not necessary to retreat to the claim that the perceiver *invents* the perceived environment. However, as these historical illustrations show, the nature of the discriminations that are made can change. They relate critically to the manner in which we represent reality to ourselves. It is in this sense that perception can be referred to legitimately as constructive.

Perceptual learning and the reader

What do these views of visual perception imply for reading? One immediate consequence is that we need to reconsider the way we interpret a failure to make a particular discrimination – even one which is 'self-evident' to another observer. For example, if a child continually confuses the letters 'p' and 'q' does this failure relate to an uncorrected optical defect? Fairly obviously not, since the consequences of such a defect would have become apparent much earlier in the child's interaction with objects. Why, then, cannot the child see what is before its eyes? The question is a familiar one. In fact, in the light of the argument presented so far, and bearing in mind the examples of 'theory-driven' perception, we need not see the failure as particularly puzzling at all. If unique responses are not attached to the letters 'p' and 'q', this means that the child has no theory about their difference, *not* that the difference cannot be seen. The letters are *functionally* equivalent, and the apparent perceptual failure can be recognized for what it is: a *conceptual* deficiency. The letter 'p', for example, is but one token of a very large number of symbols which by a slow learning process come to activate the idea 'letter p'. It is not difficult to appreciate that this mental work may, at some early stage, fail to make use of the one feature that we identify as allowing for the discovery of another idea, namely, 'letter q'. This example is particularly pertinent since it points to a conflict between the child's normal experience of the world and the visual experience of reading. In the real world mirror reversals are very common. For example, the child must learn that the view from both sides of an object, although reversed, does *not* signal distinct objects at all.

The business of teaching a child to read involves, in part, making clear what are the relevant distinctions. It follows therefore that two quite peculiar problems arise: (1) the teacher's categories will not necessarily be shared by the child. As we have seen, this is not simply to claim the child *knows* less; it means that teacher and pupil *see* the world in different ways. (2) the process of teaching itself involves bringing the child to an awareness at a *general* level of certain theoretical ideas. Teacher and child need to evolve a language which can be used to discuss the process of learning. We shall take up the implications of this second point later.

With regard to the first point some interesting data of Eleanor Gibson can be cited. She considered a set of nine letters which could (from the adult's point of view) clearly be categorized on a number of visual features. Thus letters were used which were straight-sided, curved, contained diagonals or used vertical lines. All possible pairs of letters were presented to groups of children and adults with the instruction to decide whether the letters comprising each pair were the same or different. Errors on this task can be taken as a measure of how easily confused two letters are. The time taken to make correct decisions can be used in a similar way: difficult judgements take longer.

The results of this study can be summarized in the form of a diagram such as that shown in Figure 3.6. The analysis provides a description of the features which were used in making the decision. The main division in the diagram shows the most important distinction, with a progression of other, more detailed distinctions following. Figure 3.6(a) shows the results of a group of adults. Clearly, the most important conceptual distinction is between letters which contain a diagonal element (M, N and W) and all others. The branch on the left then shows a distinction between curved and straight letters (CG versus EFPR). The results for a group of children (Figure 3.6(b)) are rather strikingly different. For these readers the most important distinction is

(a)

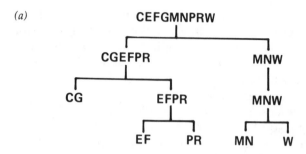

(b)

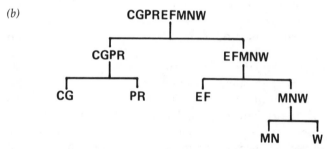

Figure 3.6   The classification of nine letters by child and adult. The pattern in (a) illustrates the features used by adults. The pattern in (b) shows the features used by children. Data from Gibson, E. J. (ed.) (1970) 'The Ontogeny of Reading', *American Psychologist*, 139 (© 1970 by the American Psychological Association; adapted by permission of the publisher and author).

between straight and curved letters (CGPR versus EFMNW).

What can be concluded from this study? Possibly, that the concepts of what it takes to make a letter are differently organized in the memories of adult and child. Different priorities attach to particular defining features. What is self-evident for the adult is not so for the child.

What the results suggest is that learning to distinguish one letter from another involves discovering which properties of any particular letter remain present in all representations. For example, what it takes to make a 'p' could be 'a vertical line with a closed curve to its right placed more than half way up'. This will be recognized as a process analogous to that involved in relating a particular acoustic signal to the set of phones. Again, there may be no *single* identifiable feature which will always signal – for example, the idea 'letter p' – but, as in the case of phone detection, this does not mean that the problem is insoluble. There are *sets* of features which, taken together, do provide enough evidence for reliable identification. If the effects of surrounding context are added (these effects are nothing more than the solutions of other detection problems) then identification becomes more certain. This is not because the physical stimulus itself becomes more discriminatable, but because confident identification is made easier when the number of alternatives possible is reduced.

The processes of perceptual learning as applied to beginning reading should be seen as the gradual construction of more and more successful ways of detecting just those features (and no others) which allow letters to be matched to their conceptual representations. But the analysis of letters goes only so far. Reading is not spelling; in normal circumstances the reader must aim to identify words, not letters alone. In fact, there are potentially a number of higher levels of organization the reader could use, including the phrase or even the sentence as a whole. The three chapters comprising the second section of the book take up these cognitive questions.

Part II
Cognitive factors

4
The meaning of words

Sounds and letters

Learning to read, in our culture at least, always involves an initial stage of looking at print and then speaking aloud. Reading is introduced to the schoolchild as an activity in which printed letters are related to speech. By the middle years of schooling this habit of reading out aloud lapses, although implicit speech may be involved in the production of writing for much longer. Relating sequences of letters to particular sounds is, therefore, the skill that must be learned first.

This chapter is concerned with the rules governing this complex activity. It is important to note, however, that another related question has been set aside for the time being. This concerns the degree to which reading is *necessarily* speech-based. There are, as everyone knows, two broad schools of thought on the question of teaching a child to read. One draws on the links with speech, the other refers to the essentially visual aspects of reading. This distinction between *phonics* and *look–say* techniques is useful, but can be overstated. As we have seen in Part I there can be no doubt that the evolution of an alphabetic writing system yielded an efficient way of depicting some aspects of speech. But we should not forget that to *depict* means to provide a visual or pictorial signal. Thus, although it would be silly to seize on the purely visual properties of words and forget the alphabetic nature of our script, words *do* have shapes and forms of their own. We shall discuss first the rules that relate letters to sounds. The question of whether they are always applied, and in what circumstances, can be left till later.

Written English contains correspondences between sequences of letters and their associated sounds. For example, all fluent readers presented with the nonsense word *strondle* will produce roughly the same pronunciation of it. How is this achieved? We can begin by taking the simplest theory: that there is one sound, and one only, attached to each of the twenty-six letters of the alphabet. From this point of view, as the reader looks at each letter of a word the appropriate sound arises in the mind as a unique event. The individual sounds can then be blended together to form an appropriate pronunciation of the word. There is a great deal wrong with this theory. In the first place, it is patently not true to say that each sound has its own unique letter. Some sounds are given by more than one letter (for example, the /s/ sound in 'circle' and 'sister'). Some letters lead to different sounds in different contexts (for example, the two instances of the letter 'g' in 'Angela's anger'). Further, particular combinations of letters at times produce sounds not obviously related to the sound of either when used in isolation (for example, 'th', 'ck', etc.). The idea that the sounds are blended in such cases appears awkward, if not ludicrous. The simple truth is that a one-to-one assignment of sound to letter will not work for English, because there are many more possible sounds than there are letters.

A second difficulty arises from the suggestion in Chapter 3 that *both* the letter and the word are possible units used in decoding writing. There are parallel considerations with regard to sounds. The sound of a word as a whole has a quality of its own and this is only in part derived from the sounds of the individual letters. Words spoken accurately have their own characteristic rhythm and intonation. A serious difficulty is presented to our simple theory by this fact. Letter sequences must not only yield up particular sounds in isolation, but also signal appropriate patterns of sound (stress patterns) depending on their context. If we assign one sound to each letter, and one only, we are left with no way of varying sounds to take account of neighbouring letters. Yet the reader clearly does do this. For example, the initial portion of the words 'photograph' and 'photography' are identical, yet this sequence of identical letters gives rise to quite different sound patterns.

A final difficulty arises when we consider the way in which the reader's eyes scan words (this is discussed further in Chapter 7). Fluent readers do not even look at all the letters of a word, and those which are looked at may not be scanned in the order in which they appear in the word. Thus, in the face of all these problems, the theory that knowing the sounds of the letters will invariably lead to the correct pronunciation of words must be abandoned. We must look for a more plausible alternative.

English spelling

Given the notorious irregularity of English spelling we might be inclined to say that no systematic rules could possibly embrace all the countless exceptions with which the beginning reader must contend. Some letters are 'silent' in contexts where simple application of spelling-to-sound rules might encourage their pronunciation. The letter 'b', for example, in words such as 'plumb', 'bomb', 'climb', 'dumb'; the letter 'k' in 'knight'; and 'g' in 'gnaw'. Words such as 'one', 'four' or 'sword' are pronounced in a way that conflicts wildly with the pronunciation of their component parts, 'on', 'our' and 'word'. Other words, such as 'ought', 'bough' and 'yacht', seem so gratuitously complicated that they are the despair of native speaker and foreigner alike. There are many reasons for these various idiosyncracies of spelling. Some relate to historical factors: the form of a word in contemporary English may owe something to its Latin, Greek or Saxon origin. Some oddities of spelling reflect no more than the whim of an influential early printer. Faced with this chaotic situation we could well be tempted to adopt the position that learning to read English is little different from learning Chinese.

We might as well forget that any relationships exist between spelling and sound, and treat each word as a visual form which stands for its meaning. There is something of an irony here. Having evolved an extremely powerful writing system capable of representing speech, it appears that we are compelled to treat its products like primitive pictograms. Fortunately, such pessimism is not completely justified. We do, however, need to look more carefully at what a writing system has to do.

To many, the issue appears straightforward. Surely, it is argued, the writing system must signal the appropriate pronunciation of words. From this starting point the word 'bomb' must be judged as perversely spelled; it should be re-written as 'bom'. But if we do this, an unexpected difficulty arises. We lose the *physical* resemblance in the written forms of 'bomb' and 'bombardment'. In a similar way, to remove the 'b' from 'climb' is to lose the link to 'clamber'. These apparently well-motivated revisions to spelling remove the physical signs of a 'family resemblance' existing between particular groups of words. An alphabetic writing system is clearly a means for representing speech. However, reading need not be thought of as simply the process in reverse. The task facing the reader (that is, the normal fluent adult reading silently) is to understand the writer's *meaning*. There is no requirement to speak. Being able to say what has been written is a secondary, and rather less important activity. In some senses, in fact, it gets in the way. All readers (even those learning the skill) are already able to speak and understand speech. This is a very important fact, for it means that specific rules for the written form are unnecessary because the rules for pronouncing English, which all of us know, predict the appropriate way of saying what is written. *So long, that is, as the reader knows what is written.*

It is this dilemma that is at the heart of the contrast between *phonics* and *look–say* teaching methods. If a child can be taught somehow that the printed sign *carrot* refers to the familiar red vegetable served hot for dinner there is no need to learn, in addition, how to say the word. Children already know what carrots are. The problem is, how do we get the printed sign identified in the first place? We really cannot expect a child to learn all possible words as unique visual shapes. The answer lies in the alphabetic nature of our writing system. The rules relating letter and sound are, quite obviously, very imperfect, but if they can be used simply to get at the meaning of what has been written, then the question of how a word is actually spoken is solved. The child already knows. The rules relating letter and sound, therefore, ought *not* to be thought of as rules for speaking. They are, rather, a very economical way of getting at the meaning of a word. In this sense anything that will aid the reader should be retained. The fact that groups of words, although spoken differently, have a certain family resemblance of meaning is of considerable help here.

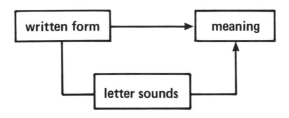

Figure 4.1   Two possible routes to meaning: directly using recognition of visual form and indirectly via coded sound.

We must conclude that there are two ways in which a written form can lead to understanding. These are illustrated in Figure 4.1. The first is direct. By this route the visual form of a word (that is, its shape and its component letters) can be used to activate an area of the reader's knowledge. (We shall look in more detail in the next section at what this involves.) Clearly, for this route it is helpful, though not necessary, if words that address the same mental domain have visual features in common. The second route is indirect and capitalizes on the fact that there are correspondences – albeit rather weak ones – existing between letters and sounds. The sounds of letters and groups of letters can be used to get at meaning.

The two routes shown in Figure 4.1 coexist; that is, both can be used simultaneously. However, the balance between them alters very radically as the reader's fluency improves. For the adult, it is likely that the direct, visual route is used almost exclusively. For the child, on the other hand, reading is very much tied up with the *production* of speech. Inevitably this leads to an emphasis on written forms as coding speech sounds. The process of learning to read fluently involves gradually abandoning this practice in favour of one which treats the printed form of words as directly accessing meaning.

The mental lexicon

We have proposed that the printed forms of words serve to activate the reader's knowledge. We must begin to make this rather vague idea more explicit. Some of the essential concepts have already been discussed in the first three chapters, where it was proposed that drawings of objects give rise to mental

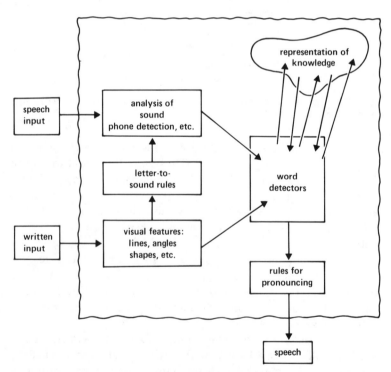

Figure 4.2 A schematic model of some features of lexical memory. Adapted from Morton, J. (1970) 'A functional model for memory', in D. Norman (ed.) *Models of Human Memory*, New York: Academic Press.

representations. The written form of words can be treated as a special type of drawing. Our knowledge of words, their physical form and their use, is as much part of our system of concepts as knowledge of objects like trees and cows. We have already discussed how features of objects are selected and used in a drawing as representations of the object as a whole. The meaning of a word is arrived at in a roughly similar way.

For our purposes we shall consider all information about words and their meaning as organized in one complex mental structure – a mental lexicon. The essential components of such a system are shown in Figure 4.2, which can be looked on as an elaboration of the ideas set out in Figure 4.1. The wavy line indicates the boundary between events in the real world and hypothesized . mental processes. Some of these latter have already been dealt with (for example, the way speech sounds are analysed). Central to the theory is the notion of a word-detector. This is a very important concept and worth considering in detail.

When we learn what a tree is, or a cow, we establish ways of identifying aspects of what we are looking at. These are just those properties or features which serve to distinguish the object from something else (a bush, for example, or a bull). It is these critical features which a drawing depicts, using the conventions of graphical representation. Once we know what a cow is we can carry out a series of 'tests' on the visual world (these are not, of course, conscious or deliberate). If we had to describe such tests they would take the form of a series of questions. For example, has it got legs? Has it got horns? Has it got an udder? If enough of these tests are 'passed' the object is identified. A drawing makes the job simpler to the extent that the defining features may be the only ones present. When we say a *word* has been learned we mean that entirely analogous mental processes have been established. That is, a series of tests adequate to distinguish one written form from others have been set up. Now, clearly, the way a word can be written varies very widely. It may be printed or handwritten, in upper or lower case, and in any one of a number of different scripts. These differences, however, do not obscure an essential identity in all the forms of any particular word, any more than differences between oaks and fir trees obscure the fact that both are trees. In the case of written words the perceptual tests relate to its visual form: the sequence of letters, for example. A word-detector can be looked on as a mental structure that simply accumulates evidence; that is, adds up the number of tests that are passed. When sufficient evidence has been collected a critical point is reached which might be termed the *threshold* of the detector. Reaching this threshold is the mental equivalent of identifying a word. It is worth stressing again that none of these processes involves conscious deliberation. Only when the threshold is passed does the reader become aware of the identity of a word.

Is it pertinent to ask what is meant by becoming aware? Although this is a very profound question, raising many issues, for our purposes it can be dealt with quite simply. We need to distinguish what we know from what we are conscious of. Obviously, we all possess a vast amount of information. This is coded in the brain in a form that allows us to get access to particular parts without continually being aware of everything. You can, for example, as you read this sentence decide to stop thinking about reading and think instead about fungus diseases of goldfish. The printed words serve to bring into consciousness a new train of thought. A word can do this because part of what we know about it is its physical form. The mystery is that this very *particular* knowledge gives rise to a process that is not at all particular – it is, in fact, a potentially endless process. What we know about any single word is capable of almost indefinite elaboration. Psychological insight into the mechanisms controlling this process has so far been very slight. Some rather general proposals can, however, be made.

It can be seen in Figure 4.2 that word-detectors connect with the stored representations of meaning in a two-way fashion. Once a word-detector has been activated particular meanings are evoked. This process then leads to changes in the thresholds of other word-detectors. The changes can be in two directions: a threshold may be lowered so that less evidence is needed for identification, or it may be raised. In this way, as reading progresses, the organization of the reader's knowledge becomes imposed, in a very general way, on the word-detectors themselves. The meaning of what is read does not reside in the printed words, but in the knowledge which they evoke. In fact, a large number of words are ambiguous, yet the reader is rarely aware of this. The word 'shed', for example, conveys by means of the same four letters a verb relating to the fall of leaves, or a hut. For the reader, however, the fact that these ideas share the same set of letters is quite incidental. The point is that the two conceptual domains are widely separated since knowledge is organized to reflect the structure of some part of the real world – a world in which the two meanings of 'shed' have almost nothing in common. Only one meaning, therefore, will normally survive. Which one will depend on how easily falling leaves or huts can be incorporated into the reader's train of thought. We can only speak of this awareness of meaning in metaphorical terms, as a conscious flow of ideas or images.

There are two further important properties of word-detectors: both relate to the threshold. The first is the basic level of the threshold. Detectors differ in the amount of evidence they need. The most important influence here is the familiarity of the word – how frequently it is encountered. Words that are frequent in the written language are more easily detected. This is not a property of the word as such: frequently-occurring words have no distinctive physical features (they are not all short, for example). It is, rather, that for these words the detector becomes active on less evidence. There is a price to pay for this in terms of occasional misperceptions – when a detector with a very low threshold becomes inappropriately active. One particularly frequent word is the printed form of our own name. This allows for its very rapid identification in a list or directory, for example, but also leads quite frequently to misperceptions and mistakes. The second factor relates to more short-term changes in threshold. Once the threshold for a detector has been passed, it is, for a brief period, more easily activated again; its threshold is temporarily lowered. For example, if the detector for the word 'apple' has recently been active (that is, a string of letters 'apple', 'APPLE', 'aPpLe', etc. has been encountered) its resting state will change. The detector is 'primed' and will, for a period of time, need less evidence to become active again. Word-detectors can, as we have seen, be primed as a result of influences from the reader's knowledge. In fact, priming processes of this kind play a vital role in regulating the flow of ideas from text. (This point is considered in detail in Chapter 5.)

It is important to appreciate that the input to any word-detector is very rarely in an ideal form – indeed, that itself would be hard to define. The physical features defining a particular word result from the process of perceptual learning. Since these are so complex, the series of tests defining a particular detector will rarely all be passed. Several word-detectors will become active to some degree, and some may in fact become active inappropriately, although in normal circumstances only those ideas which fit the current understanding ever become conscious.

Spelling and speech

We can now return to the original problem posed by the irregularity of English spelling. The way out of this dilemma is to appreciate that gaining access to the mental lexicon gives rise to the awareness of *meaning*. It does not necessarily lead to the pronunciation of a word. Figure 4.2 shows how speech is produced. The intention to speak serves to activate the mental lexicon which, in turn, leads to speech via the application of the rules relating to how words are pronounced. These are known (by definition) by all speakers of a language. Figure 4.3 summar-

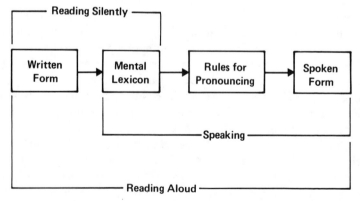

Figure 4.3   Reading silently and reading aloud contrasted.

izes these ideas. It can be seen that entries in the mental lexicon act like a bridge between writing and speech. Written text can give rise to conscious experience without speech. A particular idea can lead eventually to speech without any written input. There is, therefore, no direct one-to-one correspondence between a particular written form and a particular pronunciation. There need not be, because all native speakers know the appropriate pronunciation of words in their vocabulary.

It would perhaps be helpful to illustrate these ideas with specific examples. All speakers of English recognize that the letters 'nat' in the words 'nature' and 'natural' are pronounced differently. At the same time, if we know the language at all, we know that the two words have much in common in terms of their meaning. The similarity in spelling is a pointer to the similarity of meaning; it would be lost if separate spellings were adopted. In fact, the way the first vowel in 'nature' and 'natural' is pronounced is something determined by the rules of pronunciation. The words are spoken appropriately long before they can be read. There is no need in this case to have different ways of writing the words 'nature' and 'natural' just because they sound different. In exactly the same way, there is no need to represent two different forms of the letter 't' in the words 'resident' and 'residential', since there is a rule of pronunciation known to all speakers that will generate the appropriate change in sound. (If you doubt the existence of this rule try reading the nonsense words 'paridont' and 'paridontial'.)

The implications of this theory are rather startling. Spelling reforms that explicitly seek to signal changes in pronunciation like those mentioned are misguided since they tend to blur significant similarities in *meaning*. We are led to the conclusion that English spelling, far from being outlandishly irregular, may be quite effective in giving the reader just the kind of information needed to arrive at the *meaning* of words. There is little point in hoping to gain a large advantage for the reader by adjusting spelling to indicate all variations in sound. In fact, spelling reform along these lines is really quite unnecessary for the fluent speaker, since what would be gained would be redundant (that is, already known) and what would be lost would be many helpful visual clues to meaning.

Some implications for teaching

The educational implications of all this are complex and sometimes paradoxical. The child, faced with written letters for the
first time, will probably arrive at a belief that spelling indicates
sound. However, this hypothesis is, for practical purposes,
invalid. The way a word is spelled *can* be made to relate to part of
the child's knowledge, but not necessarily to its understanding
of how to speak. The idea of entries in a mental lexicon can be
used as a way of indicating that many words form 'families'
based on resemblances of meaning. The child can gain an
advantage from this proposition by coming to understand that
spelling is not wholly irregular or arbitrary, but relates with
some regularity to knowledge. It is rather doubtful whether
anyone would attempt to teach such ideas overtly, but it is at
least important to ensure that the child quite rapidly learns to
invalidate the hypothesis that print leads directly to sound, since
patently letter sequences (spelling patterns) are highly irregular.

Of course, if the child can gain some idea of what sort of
information the spelling patterns *do* convey the advantages
secured would be very great since, by the time the child comes to
read, the rules of pronunciation are already well known. Few
children have difficulty in pronouncing appropriately (and
understanding) pairs of words such as 'photograph'/
'photography', 'telegraph'/'telegraphy', 'courage'/'courageous',
etc. The fact that these words look similar mirrors the fact that
they are closely related in meaning. Once their meaning is
known, their pronunciation is not a problem.

It can now be seen that many difficulties stem from the fact
that, in the initial stages of reading, the child must read aloud.
Reading aloud *demands* the use of the rules of pronunciation,
whereas reading silently need not. Spelling patterns have
evolved to preserve similarities in meaning between words that
reflect aspects of the same idea. The step of actually pronouncing
words is not necessary for their understanding and is, or course,
something that the fluent reader soon learns to abandon. We
shall consider later the question of methods of teaching reading,
but it will now become very apparent why the technique of en-
couraging speech production, vocabulary enlargement and word-
play generally is *vital* rather than incidental to the task facing

the beginning reader. By these means the child may become aware of the lawful nature of the rules of pronunciation. This raising to consciousness is in part what the teaching process is about – letting the child develop a strategy based on the realities of its language. To achieve this will involve devising a way of talking about language itself: what might be called a *meta-language*. Obviously this cannot occur in a formal fashion, but it is necessary, at least, to present enough evidence to the child for relevant inferences to be made. How speech plans are realized is something to be discovered. It lies within the competence of all normal human beings and is mastered in the first two years of life. Writing and reading are, by contrast, inventions, and it is important to understand at what level these man-made skills impinge on linguistic knowledge. As we have seen, writing systems developed as methods for conveying speech, but the forms of representation that have evolved also reflect (perhaps inevitably) the organized nature of human knowledge; that is, the manner in which reality has been encoded and stored in memory. All languages capture the perceived organization of the world; not only the world of tangible objects, but of relationships and movements in space and time. Quite often representations in the mental lexicon capture these family resemblances as a direct result of the origins of writing itself. It is not, then, absurd to say that the manner in which words are written for the reader are more regular than is often claimed. The problem for the teacher is to establish that written forms can point directly to the domain of ideas – that print, albeit that it represents speech, may activate ideas without involving actual or implicit speech. Another way of making the same point is to assert that the knowledge we possess about words is very broad, and includes such things as how they are spoken, how they look, and how they relate to each other and to aspects of the world: that is, what they *mean*.

The coding of sound

The careful reader will have detected a problem with this analysis. If written words serve to access meaning, and part of that meaning is a representation of how to pronounce the word, how is it that strings of letters which are *not* words can be pronounced at all? To return to our original example, how is it that the string of letters 'strondle' can be pronounced? It is clearly absurd to imagine that there is an entry in the mental lexicon for all possible sequences of letters – both words and non-words. One way out of this problem is to appreciate that there are, in fact, sequences of letters in English that are recognized immediately as non-words, for example, the sequence 'xkqlr'. Impossible words like this cannot be pronounced. On the other hand, letter sequences such as 'mide' are recognized as *possible* words – that is, we would not be too surprised to discover that a 'mide' is a tool used by bricklayers, or that the verb 'to mide' means to weep. These intuitions possibly account for the fact that fluent readers may attempt to pronounce these non-words. It could be achieved in two ways. First, by analogy: there are words that are very close in their physical form to 'mide' (e.g. 'wide'). The non-word could be pronounced by analogy with this real word. To put it more exactly, the non-word could be taken as a very 'noisy' input to the word-detector for 'wide', with the reader aware that a mismatch has in fact occurred; that is, the situation is different from a mere misprint. The second method is rather more interesting. Part of the reader's knowledge relates to the correspondences between written letters and their sounds. This is shown in Figure 4.2 as a set of letter-to-sound rules. These could be applied to a non-word to produce a possible pronunciation. On balance, however, it is unlikely that such a process occurs for non-words of more than one syllable. Consider the sequences of letters 'mather' and 'mathead'. Both are non-words but the letters 't' and 'h' are, generally, pronounced differently in each. The analogy explanation would account for this well (links with 'father' and 'fathead'), but the fact that the letters are segmented quite differently is a problem for the rules of pronunciation account.

The meaning of words

Word-detectors are neutral with regard to the sort of evidence they will accept; *any* property of a word may serve to increase the activity of a detector and be treated as evidence. In this sense the meaning of a word is not a property to be detected, rather it is the end-product of the detection process. The effect of the reader's knowledge is to alter the amount of evidence needed. Thus, if we wish to ask how the meaning of words is represented we must look at the organization of knowledge itself.

Obviously, we beg an important question by setting out this way. It could be that knowledge is not organized at all or, at least, not in a way that we can understand. It is, however, worth tackling this question if only because one of our more compelling intuitions is that our knowledge *is* structured. That is, if we reflect on what we know about anything we conclude that our knowledge exists on different levels: it varies from the very particular to the general. We know, for example, that an apple is a particular kind of edible object with its own unique taste. But we also know, at another level, that many things true of apples are also true of other things: for example, they are round, hard, belong to the category fruit (and hence are related to pears, strawberries and oranges), and so on. The important psychological question is the extent to which this intuition about levels of knowledge is a reflection of the way the mind is structured. To put the question simply: is knowledge itself organized, or is it the case merely that we have developed ways of operating on what we know – habits of thought – which lead us to group things together?

If we decide to treat knowledge as being inherently organized it will soon be evident that we are on a familiar road. It was just this assumption that motivated Bishop Wilkins in his search for an ideal form of writing. We are faced with defining the fundamental categories of thought. There have been two recent and influential attempts at this question, and we shall examine them in turn.

The first is a theory of meaning proposed by two linguists, Katz and Fodor. Their theory rests on the proposition that the meaning of a word is not a unitary thing, but is made up of a number of fundamental components. These components are the 'atoms' of meaning from which all knowledge is made. It follows that they are properties which are, in general, shared between words. An obvious example is the fact that 'tree', 'donkey' and 'spider' all share the attribute 'animate'. In contrast, 'desk', 'car' and 'shoe' all make use of the component 'inanimate'. Properties like 'animate', 'human', 'male', 'hard', etc. are of great generality: they are shared between vast numbers of words. Thus, if this theory is correct, a correspondingly massive economy in representation would be achieved if, rather than specify all meanings as unique and individual, they could be dealt with as combinations of a much smaller number of basic units. (We shall consider later why economy of this kind might be a good thing.)

The features, or atoms, we have considered so far have one further property: they are all binary. That is, they refer to 'either–or' states: a thing is either animate or inanimate; male or female. Katz and Fodor went a step further and proposed that some properties were more fundamental than others – they could, in fact, be arranged in a hierarchy. The theory concentrated on one common type of word in English, namely, words with two or more meanings. They are of interest because the meaning that is arrived at depends on the particular combination of attributes used. Figure 4.4 shows this more clearly. It can be seen that the properties that will disambiguate the word bachelor (which actually has four meanings, though two are

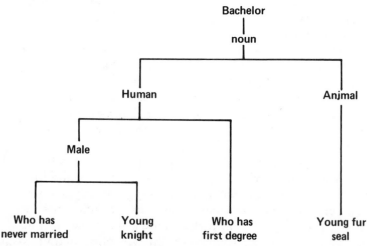

Figure 4.4   Meaning represented as components. The 'atoms' of meaning in this case serve to disambiguate the four senses of the word *bachelor*. Adapted from Katz, J. and Fodor, J. (1963) 'The structure of a semantic theory', *Language*, 170–210.

rarely used) can be set out in the form of a hierarchy. The diagram, in fact, shows two kinds of information: general properties, like 'male'; and specific detail, like 'who has first degree'. This division is an admission of the fact that not all of the meaning of a word can be extracted from components it shares with others. Some part of meaning appears to be unique.

The theory has the merit of being explicit. As a result, we can see that it fails to avoid the problems that frustrated the development of an ideal writing system. We are face-to-face with the same question: what are the essential defining properties? At an intuitive level we have no difficulty accepting a property like 'animate'. This is clearly of great generality. In fact, that is the problem: so many words share this property that it does not take us far in terms of definition. Other properties seem to be shared by so few words it seems hardly worth the trouble elevating them to the status of an atom. How do we draw the line between what is unique and word-specific and what is a general property? If the theory is to work the line must be drawn, but so far there have been no satisfactory suggestions as to how or where.

This theory – and all those like it – has to face other difficulties. For example, not all likely candidates for the status of atom are binary. Some, like colour, call for many values rather than just two. In fact, even binary properties take various forms. Some clearly involve a two-way division, like 'animate–inanimate', but others, like 'tall' and 'short' appear to exist on a continuum. They are graduated rather than dichotomous, and in their use they are *relative*. A tall dog is not taller than a short giraffe. This apparently trivial observation is ominous for the theory as it stands. If meaning really does consist of aggregates of basic atoms it is hard to see how relative properties like this can be dealt with. The theory becomes contradictory and pointless if properties high up in the hierarchy have to take account of the object to which they are applied before we can establish which value ('tall' or 'short', for example) to apply.

Thus, a considerable question mark hangs over this kind of theory. None the less, it might be objected that the difficulties we have put in its way have all been somewhat theoretical. It is still worth considering an attempt to deal with such a theory in psychological terms. The most influential account of this kind was proposed by Collins and Quillian. They argued that, notwithstanding the difficulties, a 'componential' theory of meaning has one overwhelming advantage in psychological terms: it allows for an economical storage of information. It is important to see what this 'cognitive economy' involves. Collins and Quillian were not primarily concerned with the *capacity* of the human brain. They were well aware that this is, for practical purposes, infinite. But economy of representation possibly has a part to play in the manner in which human beings think. Thought, as we have seen, can occur with differing degrees of specificity. The word 'canary', for example, can lead to the idea of something that flies. This is a fairly non-specific attribute: it is true of many birds. The word could also give rise to quite specific knowledge – for example, that its feathers are yellow. Collins and Quillian proposed that these dispositions of thought arise as a direct consequence of the organization of knowledge. Information common to all birds is stored at a higher level in the structure than features that are unique to canaries. Figure 4.5 captures

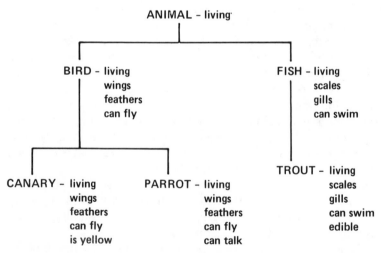

Figure 4.5 Memory representation as a hierarchical structure. Adapted from Collins, A. M. and Quillian, M. R. (1972) 'How to make a language user', in E. Tulving and W. Donaldson (eds) *Organisation of Memory*, New York: Academic Press.

some of the essential features of this proposal. The fundamental similarity to the theory of Katz and Fodor is apparent: in particular, the crucial proposal that knowledge is organized hierarchically.

Collins and Quillian argued that their theory was psychologically accurate because it made sense of certain observations. These relate to measurement of the time taken to make decisions about properties of objects. The proposition *a canary is yellow* is processed faster than *a canary is a bird*. That is, people can judge whether some propositions are true or not faster than others. This is, of course, entirely consistent with the theory illustrated in Figure 4.5. Specific information can be accessed more rapidly than more general information. The problem is that such results are also consistent with other, quite different, theories. For example, the result could arise as a quite trivial consequence of the fact that there are more birds than there are canaries. It might take longer to search through the larger set, but the result may say nothing about organization.

If Collins and Quillian had chosen as their example of a bird an ostrich or a penguin we would have become aware of a more fundamental problem with their approach. It is simply not true that we treat all examples of birds as, in some way, equivalent, all being grouped under a common superordinate heading. Some instances of the category 'bird' strike us as more appropriate than others. In Figure 4.6, for example, we are perfectly able to

Figure 4.6 Variations from a 'typical' bird. Adapted from Clark, H. H. and Clark, E. V. (1977) *Psychology and Language*, New York: Harcourt Brace Jovanovich.

decide that some birds are better examples of the category than others. Quite obviously, if our mental representation of a sparrow is judged to be a better example of a bird than a goose it is pointless in the first place to propose a theory in which all examples of a category are neatly organized in a hierarchy, each with the same weight. We must face the fact that human memory does not appear to work like this.

How then, is knowledge organized? Perhaps the best way of approaching the question is to consider how information is acquired in the first place. The mental processes that allow us to know that a canary is a bird are not unrelated to the perceptual processes that allow us to identify a canary as an object in the real world. That is, the 'features' of our mental lexicon – the atoms of meaning – may not be well represented as abstractions such as 'animate'. They may be closer to the units we characteristically employ when making perceptual discriminations. An example may make this clearer. Figure 4.7 illustrates some of the defining features of a cup. By examining the way distortions of various properties work we can get some intuitive grasp of what it takes to perceive an object as a cup. Moving from 1 to 4, for example, changes the relationship between the overall width and the height. We tend to categorize 4 as a bowl, not a cup. Similarly, variation in height and position of handle (from 1 to 9) changes a cup to a beaker.

The important point to note is that these various properties are not hard-and-fast. We appear to know, as a kind of prototype or ideal form, what a basic cup looks like (1). But many variations from this can be admitted to the category. We can look on the prototype as an ideal form because it passes all the perceptual tests: it is in this sense a representation of a concept. If we accept this argument it means that categories are not defined at all in the manner suggested by hierarchical theories. Knowledge consists of a series of tests on the environment: the degree to which these are satisfied has no fixed limit. Thus, it is more or less pointless to ask what defines a chair. Our knowledge in various circum-stances may allow a pile of books or a tree trunk or even a table to be admitted to the category. There is no way that these processes can be captured by using a set of hierarchically organized features.

Figure 4.7 Various cup-like objects illustrating the boundary of the concept of a 'cup'. *Source:* Labov, W. (1973) 'The boundaries of words and their meaning', in C. N. Bailey and R. W. Shuy (eds) *New Ways of Analyzing Variation in English*, Washington, D.C.: Georgetown University Press.

5
The
meaning
of
sentences

Beyond the lexicon

In Chapter 4 we considered how written words came to be seen as having meaning. Although the idea of a mental lexicon is useful, it does not take us far in establishing a theory of reading. The reader cannot arrive at the sense of a passage of organized prose simply by discovering the entry for each word in the mental lexicon. The reason for this is obviously that sentences carry a meaning of their own, achieved by the organization of individual words. There are, in fact, many words in the language that exist only to achieve this organizing quality: they do not have meanings in their own right. Thus, although we can think of possible entries in the mental lexicon for words like 'chair' or 'man', there are other words, like 'ought' or 'was', whose existence seems to depend on the fabric of the sentence. They do not easily stand alone. Indeed, we are hard-pressed to offer the definition of a word like 'was'.

This chapter is concerned with the properties of strings of

words; that is, sentences and groups of sentences. We have discussed how the reader gains access to the meaning of individual words and must now turn to the more complicated question of how unique combinations of words give rise to their own particular meaning.

We ought, from the start, to dismiss the notion that this can be achieved by somehow adding up the individual meanings of all the words in a sentence. In the first place, since so many words have multiple meanings, the end-product of such a procedure is bound to be highly ambiguous. An even more serious problem is that the structure of a sentence itself plays a part in determining its meaning. The sentence 'John kissed Mary' does not convey the meaning of all possible combinations of John, Mary and the act of kissing. It does not mean, for example, that Mary kissed John. The structure of the sentence, like the outline of a house, is something constrained by the elements that go into it – the bricks, windows and doors – but not wholly determined by them. A house has a shape of its own which can be described by the plans which were used to build it. Similarly, a sentence has its own shape, and the description of this structure – under the term *syntax* – has occupied linguists for many centuries. There is, as we all know, an elaborate set of terms for describing syntax. The elements of grammar, which so preoccupied the schoolchild of fifty years ago, describe the structure of the sentence using terms such as subject, predicate, noun-phrase, verb, complement, and so on. What we need to consider here is the psychological significance of these descriptions: we need to account for the way the reader understands a sentence.

Linguistic intuitions

The first point to be made is that one need not know the vocabulary of formal syntax to be aware of the structure of sentences, any more, that is, than one needs the plans of a house to be able to live in it. All readers are exquisitely sensitive to the structural niceties of what they read. There is a neat demonstration of this fact in an experiment carried out by Levelt (1969). Normal readers (that is, not trained linguists) were given the task of reading a sentence and then making judgements on sets of words taken from it. All possible groups of three words were presented, and in each case the reader was asked to indicate which two seemed closer together with respect to the meaning of the sentence. For example, the sentence 'The old dog tore the slipper', might be presented, followed by all possible sets of three words, in a random order. The set 'old', 'dog', and 'slipper' would probably elicit the judgement that 'old' and 'dog' were the closest two words. It will be evident that a study like this provides results that relate each word to every other. Such data can be analysed using the technique employed by Gibson *et al.* (see Figure 3.6) to deal with letter discrimination judgements. The matrix of comparisons can be boiled down to a single diagram which encapsulates in one structure all the judgements made. The method is ideal for looking at word judgement data. It gives an insight into the way the reader has construed the structure of the sentence, and allows us to draw a plan of this mental model. Since we can simultaneously show how each word relates to every other we can map out the reader's private syntax. The results of Levelt's study are impressive. As Figure 5.1 shows, judgements of words taken from a sentence reproduce very well the formal descriptions that a linguist would provide to

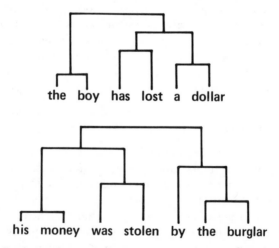

Figure 5.1   Reader's judgements of the structure of sentences. Data adapted from Levelt (1969).

describe its syntax. In other words, it would appear that this structural knowledge is part of the repertoire of skills that all normal readers possess. In most cases it is, of course, implicit knowledge, in contrast to the explicit descriptions the linguist can provide. But we are less concerned with whether the reader has a terminology for *describing* syntactic knowledge as with the existence of the knowledge itself. Results like those in Figure 5.1 show beyond doubt that all readers, implicitly at least, demonstrate a sensitivity to the structure of sentences.

Words in combination

We have not offered any account of *how* the reader arrives at decisions about structure. What mental processes achieve this result? The most tempting answer to this question is simply to propose that there exists a mental mechanism whose function is to produce a syntactic analysis – a kind of mental parser. The solution is attractive, but a moment's thought leads to the conclusion that very little has been actually explained by adopting it. We discussed in Chapter 2 the seductive power of linguistic ideas, and to keep faith with the principles set out there we should try to avoid elevating the linguistic theory of syntax to the status of a psychological explanation. But if we abandon the idea of a mental parser to complement the mental lexicon, how is syntactic structure analysed? The first step to answering this question is to realize that part of what is known about individual words (that is, part of what is represented in the mental lexicon) is their ability to combine with other words. For example, part of our knowledge of the word 'cry' is that it is an activity and that the actor must be animate. At a deeper level our knowledge of this activity suggests that the actor be human. Another way of describing this knowledge is to assert that 'cry' is a verb that takes an animate (human) subject. But the mental lexicon itself need not deal in such abstractions. It is a property of the world we live in that determines this knowledge: we know that babies cry and that rocks don't. The meaning of a word is, then, to be seen as a specification of its possible uses. This involves necessarily the consideration of other words, and we use syntax to describe the interconnections.

When we considered the operation of the mental lexicon we restricted ourselves to the reading of single words. When we read a single word its many potential meanings become available as a conscious experience. But when we read a series of words we are scarcely aware of these individual elements at all. Our experience is of a focused stream of thought – the orderly progression of ideas. For the fluent reader the particular words, and their particular order, that produce this train of thought can be rapidly dismissed. The key psychological question is how thoughts come to be regulated in this way. How is it that we know the meaning of a sentence and not the multiple combined meanings of its constituent words? The answer must lie in the process we described in Chapter 4 as priming: the effect that reading one word has on the accessibility of other words in the lexicon. Priming is a powerful and ubiquitous process. Gaining access to any item in the mental lexicon results in a spread of activation throughout the system as a whole.

There are numerous ways of demonstrating this spreading activation. Two are of particular interest in the study of reading. The first relates to a systematic alteration in the amount of physical stimulation needed to recognize a word. Priming means that the threshold for detection is lowered. We are willing to identify a word that has been primed on the basis of less evidence than would normally be needed. It may seem somewhat strange to speak of the detection of words that are clearly printed and in direct vision, but we shall take up in Chapter 7 the degree to which printed words do in fact meet these criteria. For the time being discussion of thresholds and priming can be deferred. The second demonstration is more direct and relates to the speed at which words can be read aloud. Other things being equal, this provides a fairly direct measure of priming. For example, the speed with which the word 'doctor' can be read aloud is reduced if a word such as 'hospital' or 'nurse' has been read previously. This is not just a function of reading *any* prior word: unrelated words such as 'table' or 'teapot' do not lead to the same facilitation. Why does this speeding-up occur? Obviously part of the answer relates to the fact that 'doctor', 'hospital' and 'nurse' are related. This relationship is not a superficial one; it is not, for example, a function of the physical properties of the words – the number of letters they contain, or the fact that they rhyme. It relates to a more fundamental property: the fact that all the words exist potentially in the same domain of knowledge. The word 'doctor' is read faster because the reader is primed to expect it. Reading a word activates a whole domain of knowledge, and the elements within this can be processed more efficiently.

Focused activation

How far has this taken us towards an understanding of the mental process underlying syntactic judgements? At first sight the theory of priming takes us further away from this goal. If words serve to prime other words, in an undifferentiated way, why do we not become overwhelmed with potential meanings as all possible sense of words spring to mind? This is a far cry from the orderly, regulated process of thought that we claimed characterized the processing of sentences. In order to face this objection we need to complicate slightly our theory of priming. This can be best done by means of an example. If the word 'shut' is read, other words become primed. In particular the words 'open' and 'closed' both become more accessible. We have already discussed the reason for this: presenting the word 'shut' leads the reader to enter a domain of knowledge (in this case, possible states of objects which can be shut). Doors can be shut, as can boxes, shops and mouths. One can imagine a diffuse spread of activation relating to possible 'shut' events. Thus, the presentation of a single word may prime words of the same meaning and also opposites. Obviously this effect would be disastrous for the reader of connected prose. Our theory cannot survive if it is to predict that reading the sentence 'the door was shut' will prime the word 'open'. But note that we have not, so far, proposed that what was read *was* a sentence. We have restricted ourselves to single words, and it is, of course, merely a manner of speaking to say these are 'read': it might have been more accurate to use a term like 'uttered'. The secret of the regulatory mechanism that inhibits inappropriate thoughts lies in the combination of presented words. Even if only a *pair* of words is presented the pattern of priming changes. The phrase 'shut door', for example, will prime other adjectives relating to the state 'shut' (e.g. 'closed'), but now opposites appear not to be primed. It is intuitively easy to see why. Presentation of the pair of words leads the reader to access a domain of knowledge dealing with a particular state of affairs in the world. One way of describing this would be to say the reader has a mental model of this state of the world. Part of the conscious experience may be the formation of an image. Priming will take place, but only within the circumscribed domain that has been defined by the combination of the two words.

In the case of sentences the priming effects are even more tightly controlled. Priming takes place now only for concepts that relate to the meaning of the sentence as a whole. It is important to appreciate that this has little to do with the form of the sentence – the individual words – and a great deal to do with the state of affairs in the world that the sentence asserts. Reading the sentence 'the weather was hot' will prime a word like 'warm', but it will not prime the word 'cold', although, of course, a sentence such as 'the weather was cold' is perfectly possible in English.

Mental syntax

We can now begin to see what all this has to do with syntax. Possible combinations of words are really determined by possible states of the world. There are, to continue with the example of the last section, countless possible combinations of adjectives and nouns. All those that actually refer to a possible state of the world can be described as *legal* combinations, but what is true of all the combinations is that they can be described by the simple rule (adjective + noun). It is possible, therefore, to generalize from the word combinations a rule that (adjective + noun) is lawful in English. The reader could arrive at other similar rules – for example, that (noun + verb) or (verb + adverb) are potentially legal combinations. This notion of legality is in fact very abstract. It means the reader possesses knowledge at a higher level than the particular endless number of combinations of words. It is a form of knowledge that allows the intuition that the phrase 'the tired rock' is more acceptable than 'the quickly man'. Both are nonsense, but the first phrase conforms to an abstract rule concerning adjectives and nouns, while the second violates a rule relating to adverbs. It is possible, therefore, to have intuitions about what is grammatical quite apart from what makes sense. Making sense relates to possible combinations of ideas and this, at root, is determined by our knowledge of states of the real world. We may, however, capitalize on legal but nonsensical combinations of words to create new knowledge. This is how metaphor works, and is the reason why 'the tired rock', after a moment's analysis, becomes not so nonsensical after all.

The formal name we give to the abstract general rules that govern word combinations is syntax, but seen this way it becomes clear that there is no necessity for us to assume that such rules are *used* as psychological processes. One does not use the plan of a house in order to see its structure. In summary, it is proposed that reading sentences, as distinct from reading words in isolation, leads to a constrained pattern of excitation in the mental lexicon. It is as if the reader constructs a single meaning, a single set of referents, for what is read. Context acts to alter the end-product of the process of accessing the mental lexicon. It determines which of the innumerable senses of a particular word will endure. From the point of view of the fluent reader, this means that ambiguity at the level of the word is rarely detected. Only that sense of a word that can be adapted to the train of thought in progress will survive. Other senses will, momentarily, be activated but they will never become conscious. There is no call to become fanciful about the reasons for this. The reader's single mental construction demands attention if it is to be sustained, and human attention is a highly selective attribute. Only one sequence of ideas at a time can be the focus of attention.

Beyond the level of the word there are other potential sources of ambiguity. It is sometimes possible to organize the same set of words into two or more structures with different meanings. An example would be the sentence 'they are eating apples'. In extreme cases we may encounter sentences whose structure is not at all obvious, for example, the sentence 'the boat sailed on the pond sank'. Ambiguity at a structural level is easily dealt with in terms of the theory we have proposed. In general, only that meaning that can be assimilated to the train of ideas the text has evoked will be identified. In normal prose, if we discover sentences that demand more than one structural interpretation, and we become aware of both, the text should not simply be seen as ambiguous but as anomalous. Truly ambiguous sentences, which might be looked on as analogues of the ambiguous drawings in Figure 2.6, are simply literary oddities. Similarly, sentences that lead the reader to assign the wrong structure simply should not occur in well-formed prose. They are of some interest, of course, because, like visual illusions, they appear to offer fleeting insights into our own normally unconscious mental processes. But the comparison with visual illusions is a poor one. The visual world is, in principle, ambiguous. A written text serves to produce in the reader's mind a single, coherent set of ideas. There is no necessity for sentences to be ambiguous syntactically and we should resist the temptation of drawing strong conclusions from the study of the reader's behaviour when presented with them.

Mental constructions

We have several times introduced the idea of a train of thought or a conceptual domain without defining what these rather vague notions refer to. In this section we shall set out a way of characterizing the reader's knowledge. Perhaps the most direct definition is to suggest that sentences lead to states of mind that can be described by sets of propositions. The difference between a sentence and a proposition is of some importance. A proposition deals with what the sentence is about, rather than with the precise words used. It is, therefore, a way of stating relationships between two or more concepts. Thus, there may be many different sentences that state that 'Fred made bread' (e.g. 'the bread was made by Fred') all of them, at the level of the proposition, linking *Fred* and *bread* by means of the relationship *make*. A proposition, therefore, is a structure that holds together different parts of the mental lexicon in interaction. It is important to note that a proposition makes explicit relationships that may only be implicit in the sentence itself. Thus, the sentence 'Fred shot the albatross' may be represented at the propositional level with some reference to an instrument (for example, a gun). The answer to where this additional information comes from is, of course, that it is part of our conceptual knowledge. What we know about the verb 'shoot' is that it demands a weapon. Although not explicitly stated in the sentence, the proposition draws out this inference in representing what the sentence asserts.

As a text progresses, the web of propositions grows and elements become more densely interrelated. What gives a text cohesion – the sense that it is going somewhere – is the fact that propositions may be interconnected, by sharing relationships or concepts. It is obvious there are many ways of saying or writing the same thing: one may be terse or discursive; one may help the reader by frequent explicit cross-references or demand a greater mental effort to draw out inferences and fill in the intended sense. Whatever the means employed, the purpose of all texts is to lead to understanding. That is, the *same* understanding may be arrived at by indefinitely many *different* sets of sentences. All end up being described by the *same* set of propositions. This rather daring idea is supported by a number of psychological studies. Perhaps the most telling is the observation that the time it takes to read a passage of text does not relate directly to its length as measured by the number of words. What it does relate to, in an almost perfect fashion, is the number of propositions it contains. Another illustration is provided by the comparison of the two texts in Figure 5.2. Obviously both say the same thing but take quite different routes in doing it. The second version, in which the ideas are jumbled together, takes far longer. However, interestingly, once read, questions about the text are dealt with at the same speed and with the same accuracy regardless of the version presented. What is suggested by this result is that the propositional structure arrived at (easily in one case and laboriously in the other) was identical for the two passages.

The set of propositions is itself highly organized. Some are very specific, others are general and act to organize the body of knowledge. Psychological evidence shows that it is low-level propositions that are forgotten first. Thus, quite soon after reading a book, the reader may not be able to recall the names of characters (after all, we do not possess entries in our mental lexicon for fictional characters). After a few days all that may be

Simple:	The council of elders in the land of Syndra meets whenever a stranger arrives. If the council meets and if the stranger presents the proper gifts to the council, he is not molested by the natives. The explorer Portmanteau came to Syndra without any valuable gifts.
Complex:	The arrival of strangers in the land of Syndra, like the explorer Portmanteau, who did not bring valuable gifts, always resulted in a meeting of the council of elders, which insured that the stranger was not molested by the natives upon receipt of the proper gifts.

Figure 5.2   A simple and a complex propositional structure. *Source:* Kintsch and Monk (1972).

recalled are a few very high-level ideas. That is, we may know very generally what the book was about. What is certainly true is that memory for the precise words used in a book begins to fade almost instantly. Their function was merely to evoke appropriate concepts and establish a representation of meaning. This last appears to exist in a 'language' which owes nothing to written language as we know it. Our ideas are captured in the language of thought – what is sometimes termed, facetiously, *mentalese* – and we are some way yet from understanding the grammar of *that*.

Learning and knowing

The argument developed so far leads quite naturally to some important distinctions in the function of written texts. Some sentences *inform*, others *describe* what we already know. Some ask the reader to *learn*, others merely demand the reader's *attention*. Some texts are hard, some are easy; some entertain, and some do not. How can all these differences be characterized? In the first place, as we have already seen, the ease with which something can be read is a function of the number of propositions it contains. We might call this the *density* of the text. But even with texts of similar density, some function merely to access the reader's existing knowledge, whereas others demand the re-organization of concepts or the creation of new ones. Sometimes what we read calls for no change in our mental structures. A pulp novel, for example, can be read with pleasure and understood. However, it will leave no lasting trace. In this sense the pleasure of reading was that of idly shuffling existing concepts into a temporary organization. In contrast, there are texts whose purpose is to produce new knowledge; that is, new conceptual structures. Very little is understood of how this process occurs. What is certain is that, particularly in our early years, the way we symbolize to ourselves what we know of the world is in a rapid state of change. One of the most potent means of symbolizing is, of course, written text. In this way, writing, which began as a means for obtaining a permanent record of knowledge, can be used to turn round on itself and modify knowledge itself.

Structure and style

We have now defined the goal of reading as the construction of a set of propositions. These represent what the text asserts. They exist in a mental world of the reader's creation. The manner in which sentences are written and the order in which they appear can aid or impede the reader in the process of mental construction. It is no accident that rules of good style in writing have existed for almost as long as writing itself. Although consideration of these rhetorical principles would take us too far afield, there is at least one psychological principle of the same kind that merits our attention. This is the so-called 'given-new' contract, first introduced into psychology by Haviland and Clark in 1974. What is meant by this is that writer and reader agree implicitly to obey a convention that information can be segregated roughly into new material presented for the first time, and old, that is what the reader already knows or can infer. Why it is described as a contract is that the writer provides the reader with enough signals in the text as to what is old and what is new for the reader to process the material in an orderly fashion. The contract is in a sense a question of style, but if it is too frequently neglected the reader may become bewildered or misled and eventually conclude that no coherent message is to be extracted from the text. Any sentence will contain clues as to what it is that the reader is assumed already to know. This information is referred to as the presuppositions of the sentence. One obvious clue is the use of the definite article in a sentence of the form 'John saw the cow jump the fence'. If this appears as part of a text, the definite article in the phrase 'the cow' signals to the reader that knowledge is presupposed. We are concerned with a particular cow which will already have been established in the reader's mental model of what the text refers to. It is vital to label in this way what is already known, and distinguish it from new information which must be added to the propositional base. Thus the pair of sentences 'The car ran over a cat' and 'John took the cat to a vet' cohere. The reader is willing to accept that the cat in the second sentence refers to the same animal as the cat in the first. Something goes badly wrong if we are presented with 'The car ran over a cat' and 'John took a cat to the vet'. We are led to conclude that there are two cats (or even two events) involved here. As we have seen, it is the repetition of concepts in the propositional base (not necessarily their overt repetition in the written form of the sentences) that makes sentences cohere. The 'given-new' contract is a way of describing the helpful consequences of such repetitions. If the contract is violated in one way or another then rules of inference are brought to bear on whatever the sentence asserts. The reader struggles to make sense of what is written. *Some* propositional construction, even an implausible one, will be made. The factors influencing this mental housework are the subject of the next chapter.

6
Understanding text

Drawing inferences

We shall discuss in this chapter various ways in which the reader's knowledge and beliefs influence the interpretation of written text.

Consider the difference between these two sentences:

Last week Barbara went driving down the motorway and the police stopped her.

and

Last week Elizabeth went driving down the motorway and the police stopped her again.

The effect of the word *again* is quite remarkable. We are inclined to treat the first sentence as providing information; the second invites a number of speculations. Above all, the sentence suggests that Elizabeth is a reckless driver. However, since this is clearly not a presupposition of the sentence, it is reasonable to ask where the 'added' information came from. An obvious first place to look is, of course, at the word *again*, but we gain no more from that than the commonplace fact that the word relates to repeated events. It certainly does not, of itself, convey any information about reckless driving. We might wish to claim that the interpretation follows quite naturally: if someone is often stopped by the police on a motorway the most likely reason is that the car is being driven in a reckless way. But if we mean by this that the word *again* triggered this knowledge it is important to see that we are making a very radical proposal. We are placed in the position of claiming that understanding a sentence may not depend solely on what is written, but will also, and perhaps crucially, depend on what the reader knows. Without some knowledge of cars, motorway behaviour and the activities of the police the second sentence would not represent a statement about reckless driving. But if we are to allow the reader's inferences to govern in this way what a text means, it is reasonable to ask what limits are set on the process. How far may the reader go, and has the writer any control over the interpretation placed on what has been written? This chapter attempts to deal with these questions.

Frames of knowledge

In Chapters 4 and 5 we defined the reader's task in terms of constructing a set of propositions that represent the meaning of text. The main focus of our discussion was the meaning of words as accessed in the mental lexicon and the effect on the reader of word combinations. Our concern now is to break away from this conception and introduce a new dimension into the task of reading. The meaning of words, as agreed referents for objects and for states of the world, is perfectly satisfactory, but does not go far enough. There is a dimension to meaning which is unique to each person: this too is evoked by written script. Further, the reader's point of view colours the interpretation placed on a text. This is graphically illustrated by the passage of prose shown in Figure 6.1. This may be read from two points of view: that of a potential house-buyer, and that of a potential burglar. Readers asked to adopt the first viewpoint tend to remember elements such as the leak in the ceiling and the rotting roof; whereas those adopting the point of view of a burglar tend to recall elements such as the colour TV and the locked jewel box.

What these results suggest is that reading from a particular point of view affects the ease with which different parts of text

The two boys ran until they came to the driveway. 'See, I told you today was good for skipping school,' said Mark. 'Mom is never home on Thursdays,' he added.

Tall hedges hid the house from the road so the pair strolled across the finely landscaped yard. 'I never knew your place was so big,' said Peter. 'Yeah, but it's nicer now than it used to be since Dad had the new stone siding put on and added the fireplace.'

There were front and back doors and a side door which led to the garage which was empty except for three parked 10-speed bikes. They went in the side door, Mark explaining that it was always open in case his younger sisters got home earlier than their mother.

Pete wanted to see the house so Mark started with the living-room. It, like the rest of the downstairs, was newly painted. Mark turned on the stereo, the noise of which worried Pete. 'Don't worry, the nearest house is a quarter of a mile away,' Mark shouted. Pete felt more comfortable observing that no houses could be seen in any direction beyond the huge yard.

The dining-room, with all the china, silver and cut glass, was no place to play so the boys moved into the kitchen where they made sandwiches. Mark said they wouldn't go to the basement because it had been damp and musty ever since the new plumbing had been installed.

'This is where my Dad keeps his famous paintings and his coin collection,' Mark said, as they peered into the den. Mark bragged that he could get spending money whenever he needed it since he'd discovered that his Dad kept a lot in the desk drawer.

There were three upstairs bedrooms. Mark showed Pete his mother's closet which was filled with furs and the locked box which held her jewels. His sisters' room was uninteresting except for the colour TV which Mark carried to his room. Mark bragged that the bathroom in the hall was his since one had been added to his sisters' room for their use. The big highlight in his room, though, was a leak in the ceiling where the old roof had finally rotted.

Figure 6.1 This passage of prose can be read from the point of view of a house-buyer or a burglar. *Source:* Pichert and Anderson (1977).

are understood. Some parts of the text mesh in with pre-existing knowledge and expectations; others, while they make perfect sense, do not readily find a place in the overall representation of meaning that the reader has constructed. We can make this idea more formal by considering the reader's state of mind (that is, existing knowledge, attitudes and points of view) as a set of propositions. Figure 6.2, for example, sketches in fragments of the knowledge of a potential house-buyer and a potential burglar. It was pointed out in Chapter 5 that reading for under-

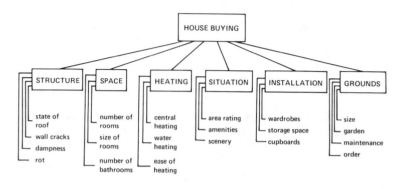

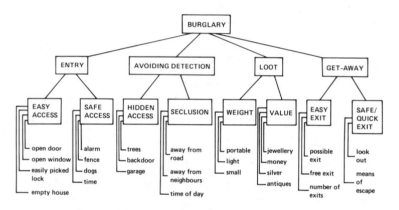

Figure 6.2   Aspects of knowledge relevant to the perspective of a 'house-buyer' or 'burglar'. *Source:* Al-Ahmar, H. F. (1983) *Some Effects of Perspectives on Reading and Recall,* unpublished Ph.D. thesis, University of Dundee.

standing involves discovering a match between some referent of the text and some part of the reader's system of ideas. In this sense reading can be looked on as a kind of mental acknowledgment that suitable referents have been found. Clearly, house-buyers and burglars will remember different aspects of the same situation. They are mentally confirming different sets of concepts and expectations.

Figure 6.2 is intended to convey part of what the reader already knows. This goes beyond representations of agreed meanings in the mental lexicon, and captures the unique sense that a particular point of view imposes. It is in this knowledge-base that the text finds an echo. It follows, therefore, that a passage of prose may give rise to a far richer set of ideas than the entries in the lexicon for individual words would suggest. We speak of the reader making inferences, but in one sense they were already made: they existed as part of the reader's knowledge. Inferences travel as undeclared baggage in the journey from text to mental representation. We may already know that policemen stop cars when offences take place. The writer can take account of this and assume the information to be known. To do this is to take a gamble on the reader's knowledge, but when we are dealing with widely understood states of the world the risk is small.

There is a parallel here with the prototype representation of objects discussed in Chapter 3. A lot of shared knowledge takes this form: it is not hard-and-fast, and is certainly not logically necessary, but represents a 'most likely' description. For example, what we know *in general* about policemen (and it is knowledge that we are all likely to share) can be set out as a collection of 'default states' representing their most likely behaviour in certain contexts. It is this knowledge that led to the inference about reckless driving. It is not *necessary*, since the sentence

> Last week Elizabeth went driving down the motorway and the police stopped her again and gave her a prize for courteous driving.

makes sense. This, however, is an unlikely event. In much the same way our prototype for a house (that is, the default state) has windows in the walls and a chimney on the roof, but we would still accept as a house an object with windows in the roof and a chimney through the wall. Knowledge of this form has fuzzy edges, not hard-and-fast limits.

While the general argument being made here might be accepted for fluent adult readers, it might be claimed that the beginning reader is much more tightly yoked to the printed word. This is a misguided view for two reasons. First, it makes an assumption that there exist certain types of text that wholly contain a specific meaning and no other. That is, it assumes there is something definite to be yoked to. To claim this is to claim that there exist texts that do not call for, or even admit, inferential processes on the reader's part. We shall propose strong reasons for questioning this idea later in the chapter. The second reason relates to a misconception about the nature of the beginning reader's pre-existing knowledge. Consider the sentence

John sat on the gate.

and contrast it with

The hen sat on her egg.

Both sentences could be found in the early pages of an introductory reader, but if they are to *mean* anything to the child, quite complex pre-existing knowledge must be evoked. This relates to the force (literally) of the word *sat* in the two sentences. To understand these sentences the reader *must* know something about the relative weight of people and hens and the relative strength and rigidity of eggs and gates. (If this point is unclear, consider the sentence

John sat on the egg.

Only if the reader has prior knowledge does this lead to an understanding that the egg is crushed.) The manner in which this pre-existing knowledge supports the interpretation of the text is identical for both child and adult.

Knowledge of space

Knowledge can be thought of as a representation of features of the world we experience. Since this is experienced in spatial terms, it follows that we have ways of representing spatial information. For example, we know not only that birds have wings, but also where, relative to the bird, the wings are attached. Our mental representations preserve, necessarily, the three spatial dimensions of the physical world. All languages are replete with terms for capturing spatial relationships (e.g. 'up', 'over', 'under', 'on', 'by', 'at', 'inside', etc.). We have discussed the reader's task in terms of constructing a set of propositions, but this is rather an awkward way of dealing with references to space. It seems more likely that the reader in this case constructs a kind of mental model. The text serves to evoke the spatial relationships in an orderly fashion because we have represented these relationships as knowledge in a form that permits inferences to be made. (It would take us too far from the theme of this book to pursue this question, but it seems likely that a mental representation other than a model, such as a set of logical relationships, would *not* be similarly as effective in allowing inferences to be drawn.) The idea can be illustrated with a concrete example. If we read

John stood on the ladder and Fred walked under it.

we know that Fred walked beneath John. This knowledge follows naturally from a mental model of the situation that preserves the necessary organization of the two people and the ladder in space. In fact, once such a model has been constructed, we may be very uncertain as to the precise form of the written sentence that led to it. Other sentences that conform to the model (that is, confirm expectations about it) may be treated as indistinguishable from the original. Thus, we may be uncertain as to whether the sentence

John stood on the ladder and Fred walked under him.

was actually presented. It is the reader's knowledge of the possible organization of objects in the world that permits this effortless process of inference. The information is not contained in the sentence presented, except in so far as this allowed such a coherent model to be constructed.

It should be noted that some aspects of spatial knowledge are *necessary* – that is, they flow necessarily from properties of the world as we know it. Thus, if we read

John was in the car. The car was in the garage.

it follows that John was in the garage. Other aspects of spatial knowledge are less constrained and the mental model constructed, while true for a particular text, may not be *necessarily* true in the same way. We shall take up this question of necessary versus optional processes later in the chapter.

Knowledge of time

We have claimed that human beings represent to themselves possible states of the world and that it is these mental structures that texts activate and symbolically manipulate. It follows, therefore, that transitions between states must also be represented. We have knowledge of temporal progression: the way things change through time. Interestingly, our language tends to code time using *spatial* metaphors: it stretches out before us, lies heavy on our hands, flies past us, etc. This sometimes makes it difficult to grasp the quite distinct properties of temporal succession. In common with spatial representation there appear to be both optional and necessary aspects. The order in which events in a narrative are presented may also reflect their temporal sequence in whatever the story refers to. For example,

John sat down. He picked up his pen. He wrote down the address. . . .

In this case the mental representation is of a succession of states, their order being derived directly from their sequence as presented. However, it is quite possible for a narrative sequence to give rise to a mental chronology that does not reflect the order in which events are mentioned. For example,

Before John left for the train he ate his dinner.

We can see that words like *before* do some of this mental work for the reader, but that is not a complete explanation. We possess a great deal of knowledge relating to possible successions of events and it is this which underpins comprehension. In some cases sequences of events are tightly constrained; that is, they are not at the discretion of the writer. For example, there is something odd about the sentence

The pencil hit the floor and then John dropped it.

if, in the sentence, *it* refers to the *pencil*. However, it is important to note that it is not quite so anomalous as sentences that violate spatial constraints. We can make the sentence 'work', for example, by imagining that there is a missing event. (For example, John picked up the pencil and dropped it again.) The way in which we represent successive states of the world appears slightly different from the way in which the states themselves are coded. They are somehow less tightly coupled. A possible explanation for this is dealt with in the next section.

Scripts

One useful way of considering our knowledge of events in time is as mental 'scripts' – a term introduced by Roger Schank and his fellow workers. A script, as its name implies, provides the means for dealing with action in particular settings, much as the script of a play gives an actor a set of words and actions to perform. A simple real-life example would be the script for buying petrol from a garage. To do this we drive to the garage, choose the grade of petrol, order it (or serve it to ourselves), check the quantity and the price, pay for it, and drive away. Some of the elements in this particular script are themselves scripts. For example, paying for something is a social encounter in which a series of events must occur in the right order (the offer of money, receipt of change, etc.). We may now see why the sentence

The pencil hit the floor and then John dropped it.

seems less anomalous than expected. What is written refers to a possible script – a possible sequence of events. If the reader identifies a missing event, it may be provided in order to make sense of the narrative stream. The source of this information is, of course, the reader's own script-like knowledge. Thus, although it is neither explicit nor elegant to write

John drove to the garage, paid for some petrol and drove off.

we gather what is meant because we can embellish what is actually written by reference to a much fuller account in the form of our knowledge of what goes on in petrol stations. So powerful is this mechanism, in fact, that readers are rarely aware of how *little* explicit information may have been provided. In fact, it is very far from being straightforward to write sentences that are completely explicit and self-contained. Lawyers spend much of their time trying to bend the English language to this end, with only partial success. We must conclude that the 'naked sentence' that means the same thing to everyone does not exist, for the simple reason that its meaning is a property of people and not of words; and people differ widely in what they know.

A script is a mental device, a way of organizing a body of knowledge in which events are organized into a sequence. In one sense it acts like a 'grammar', governing particular events and encounters. If I drive to the garage and order a haircut I am deserting the script – the event is, in that sense, 'ungrammatical'. On the other hand, a description of my driving to the garage and paying *before* I get the fuel can be understood. I have merely stretched the limits of applicability of the script somewhat. The reader must do some mental work to understand the events described.

It can be seen that the notion of a script is very powerful. It implies that the writer establishes a form of contract with the reader. Since both share knowledge of what is being discussed, a certain amount of knowledge can be presupposed or referred to in an indirect manner. The script in this way supports the process of understanding and allows sequences of sentences to be integrated. If the writer is reasonably considerate the process can be effortless. For example, the sentence

John went to the restaurant and had dinner.

establishes (with near certainty) a wealth of information in the reader's mind. Since most adults possess a script for restaurant-going, the sentence allows a great deal of information to be generated – John is indoors, is seated, has spoken to a waiter, etc. Note none of this is necessarily true. The restaurant may be an outdoor self-service barbecue, but if it is, the writer would be inconsiderate not to make this explicit early on. Otherwise, on encountering the sentence

When it started to rain he ran for shelter.

the reader will be forced to reassess the meaning of the text. The words comprising a text do not achieve their depth of meaning solely because this is represented in the mental lexicon. We must take account of the reader's interpretive processes.

Although the idea of scripts is useful, it is clear that there must be texts (and life experiences) for which no script exists. It is reasonable to ask how such situations are dealt with. The first response is that scripts may be learned. In the child they may be less elaborate, but over the course of a lifetime they may become greatly extended in range and detail. For every child there is always the first walk, that first trip in a car, the first shopping expedition. The evidence certainly suggests quite strongly that scripts are formed in such encounters. For example, initially the child's expectations may be highly specific. If a cat appears on the first walk it will be looked for on the second. The process of abstracting general properties of events (which will eventually form the framework of a script) from the welter of detail takes time.

We still need to account for our understanding of situations and texts that are totally novel. It is possible that we deal with such events by relating them to what we already know. We may, faced with a novel text describing otherwise incomprehensible events, engage in a series of mental actions. One such would be to *connect* events by the simplest means possible – for example, by attempting to identify and categorize actors and actions. In other words by attempting to discover (or plausibly invent) who is doing what, where, to whom and why. In this way, sense – of a kind – will emerge. It may not be what was intended, of course, but we are dealing here with a very inconsiderate writer who was apparently willing to pay that price. It will not have escaped attention that we may, in fact, describe this 'comprehending process' as a script itself: a kind of metascript, which can be used to wring sense from the otherwise incomprehensible. Such an idea carries with it at least one very important implication for a study of the early stages of reading, where totally novel texts occur frequently. Making sense of something involves a considerable effort. The mental effort expended in forging the necessary connections brings as its reward a coherent and meaningful representation of a text. But before the reader is likely to engage in this work two facts must be established. The first is that reading has as its goal understanding, and not something else such as arriving at the sounds of words. It may not be at all obvious to the beginning reader that this is the case. The second is the observation that narratives do, as a matter of fact, make sense. That is, the reader must be aware to some extent of the writer's intentions and must believe that a process of communication is taking place. If these two conditions are met virtually all texts will be assigned *some* interpretation.

Metaphor

We appear to have broken one of the links between text and reader by arguing that what is understood is not wholly conditioned by the words on the page, and that we must take account of an implicit contract between writer and reader. The writer is able to make certain assumptions about what the reader knows, and further may assume that this knowledge will be deployed in understanding the text. In this way the reader's willingness to go beyond what is found on the page can be usefully exploited. The most obvious example of this is the use of metaphor.

When language is used metaphorically (and in this context we shall use the term to embrace both metaphor and simile, since the psychological processes involved are identical) two sets of propositions, initially unrelated, are brought together and give rise to a new concept by means of a comparison. The two propositions must have at least one element in common and it is this repetition which invites the necessary comparison and permits a connection to be made: the two propositions are meshed together. For example, consider the sentence

The sun came out like a sword and struck me.

Several tacit comparisons are being made, in particular the phrase *came out* and the verb *struck* can both, in different ways, be used to describe the sun or the use of a sword. The duel action of these terms licenses a comparison that would not otherwise have been made. It is possible that such comparisons may become so familiar that expressions lose their strictly metaphorical quality: new levels of meaning become attached to the words employed. The phrase 'the sun beat down', for example, can now hardly be seen as metaphorical. We may spot a difficulty here. Since comparisons can be made to a virtually unlimited degree it might appear that metaphorical extension itself should be unlimited.

However, it is the *aptness* of a metaphor that governs its acceptability. This refers to the singling out of one or more highly pertinent shared attribute. Thus,

The sun came out like an apple.

strikes us as a weak metaphor simply because the sense in which an apple may be said to 'come out' does not strike us as plausible if applied to the sun. The phrase

Her eyes were like stars,

on the other hand, appears tired and banal. True, both eyes and stars twinkle, but what is missing is the novelty of the comparison. It exists on only one level and, although we are willing to make it, we remain aware of many properties of eyes and stars which are not shared. In contrast,

His brain was like a sponge.

might strike us as apt because properties and functions of brains and sponges overlap and invite comparison in a complex and interesting way.

This consideration of metaphor illustrates, in a rather extreme form, the nature of the demands placed on the reader by written text. Without a process of inference – in this case involving the identification of points of comparison in two sets of propositions – the appropriate (that is, *intended*) sense eludes us. To a lesser degree what is true of metaphorical text is true of texts of any kind. As we have seen, the sentence that can stand alone does not exist. A text does not declare its meaning in the way that a drawing does. Neither should we look on writing as a kind of code that the reader must simply learn to decipher. It is essentially a process of communication in which some part of the writer's mental life becomes available to another person; and the extent to which this is achieved satisfactorily depends on the degree to which mental states parallel to those of the writer may be evoked or constructed in the reader. Clearly this is a complex and somewhat perilous endeavour.

Pragmatics

If we are to discuss writing as a process of communication we must complicate somewhat our model of the reading process. Some consideration must be given to the way people *use* words, as distinct from the way words affect individuals. One way in which a symbol may come to stand for a concept is to be found in pictographic writing systems. Some symbols, by their nature, satisfactorily denote particular concepts. A pictographic representation of a cup, for example, conveys its meaning because it looks like a cup. The three letters 'c', 'u' and 'p' can denote the same concept, but the reference in this case is quite arbitrary. Between the limits of necessary and arbitrary association we may be able to glimpse a third possibility. Consider the way the smell of fresh coffee works as a sign for coffee itself. Obviously the association is not arbitrary: part of the idea of coffee is its smell. But it is not, strictly speaking, a necessary relationship either. The aroma of coffee is only, at best, a possible portent of the thing itself. We may ask why we treat it as a sign in this way? The answer relates to what we know of the way the world is. That is, the relationship arises as part of a wider knowledge of coffee-making and drinking.

Much the same sort of consideration enters into the interpretation of what is written. The extent to which a text makes sense is intimately bound up with the degree to which writer and reader share a common view of the world. It is to this *shared knowledge* that the term pragmatics refers. The emphasis is on the sharing. We have already seen that readers go beyond the text and draw on their general knowledge to represent its meaning. In considering pragmatics we are examining the role played by the writer in this activity: the degree to which common knowledge and beliefs can be communicated. To understand how the writer controls the reader's thought processes in this way it is necessary to sharpen the distinction between what a sentence asserts and what may be implied by it, or presupposed in it.

It is possible to work out in a purely abstract way what is meant by the assertions of a sentence. To do this we must examine the words and the way they relate to possible states of the world. However, if we do this, we should acknowledge that we are treating text as a kind of logical device. What we conclude a sentence means after such an analysis may have very little to do with what it means for a reader in real life. For example, the sentence

There was no salt in the soup.

treated as a logical assertion, simply declares that at some time a particular saltless soup existed. But for the average reader the sentence carries other meanings relating to a more general knowledge of how soups are made. If we know something about soup-making the sentence may convey the sense that the cook had omitted the salt by accident. Note, however, that there is nothing in the sentence, treated in a purely logical fashion, that could lead to this interpretation. Further, the inference that soups are made by people (cooks) itself arises from what the reader knows, rather than what the words say. In other circumstances, with other readers, the same sentence could well mean 'this was, therefore, the soup prepared by the tribe for ritual purposes, from which salt is invariably omitted'. This interpretation, too, arises from a set of beliefs by writer and reader.

We may conclude that what a text means relates crucially to the presuppositions readers have about its context: that is, the sphere of knowledge to which it applies. Readers make inferences about texts – that much is obvious – but the direction these inferences take is determined (possibly controlled) by knowledge that writer and reader share.

The philosopher H. P. Grice has pointed out that conversations between people take on a similar, 'contractual' quality. In order to communicate, both parties must be informative, truthful, relevant and unambiguous. Further, each of the contributors must believe the other to be bound by the contract. Communication breaks down if, for example, one party is untruthful. It also breaks down if either *believes* the other to be lying. Of course, in lively conversation the contract may be broken, but only in a knowing way, with appropriate verbal or non-verbal clues so that the joke may be shared.

These maxims which appear to govern effective conversation relate very closely to the contract that is tacitly entered into by writer and reader. All written texts – even those for the beginning reader – exist in a communicative context in which the writer makes assumptions about the reader's knowledge. We refer to these as presuppositions. The reader makes inferences within a particular domain of knowledge, determined in part by the writer's intention. Progress is made to the extent that this mutual contract is honoured.

Not all information in text is conveyed pragmatically. There are occasions when the reader has no interpretive options. Circumstances where this arises are of interest since they throw light on the way word meaning is represented in the mental lexicon. Consider the sentence

John dropped the glass dish.

We know that dishes break when dropped. Thus, it is pragmatically determined that the sentence implies 'and the dish broke'. Clearly, however, this conclusion is not a necessary one. It is not forced on us by some property of the verb 'to drop'. It is, rather, a conclusion derived from what we know is likely to happen. The sentence

John dropped the glass dish but it didn't break.

is not anomalous – however surprising it might be. In contrast, the sentence

John dropped the glass dish but it didn't leave his hands.

is anomalous. It would appear that the outcome (losing contact with the hands) is a component part of our representation of the verb *to drop*. It represents an invariable rule of use. In the same way, the oddity of

John kicked the ball, but not with his foot.

reveals that the verb *to kick* is represented as necessarily involving *with the foot*.

In summary, we must distinguish between pragmatically determined outcomes and ones that are logically necessary. It is important to see that the first category arises from a general knowledge of the world shared between reader and writer. The second is something defined in the organization of the mental lexicon. Pragmatic implications exist on a scale of probability, not of necessity: and probable events – even when close to certainty – remain a crucial distance away from necessity. It is for that reason that a sentence like

John jumped through the window but didn't fall.

is seen as being incongruous, but not at all anomalous. It makes sense (or can be made to make sense), in fact, solely because in the scale of *possible* events there will always exist a contingency that can make the sentence work. The manner in which this is achieved, of course, owes much to the power of script-based knowledge. We have access to a vast repertoire of scripts that can be deployed to handle incongruity. Perhaps there was a net outside the window. Certain sentences give the reader a licence to manufacture appropriate contexts. However, it is a licence that is instantly revoked by sentences such as

John jumped through the window but kept both feet on the floor.

Now we are dealing with fabric of the mental lexicon, and in this case the interpretation is not optional.

Going beyond the text

The argument developed so far may seem plausible enough. It represents a claim that what is understood, or remembered, of a text is not a verbatim message tied to the words used, but a rich mental construction borrowed in large measure from the reader's existing knowledge. There is, however, a potentially grave problem with this theory. If pragmatics play so large a part in the interpretive process, how can we ensure that it is only *legitimate* inferences which are made? For that matter, how can we ensure that only a limited number of inferences are made? To put it simply, what acts to check the reader's imagination? The problem is apparent in quite simple examples. As we have seen, the sentence

John dropped the fragile glass dish.

results in a mental model that represents the dish as broken. So potent is this suggestion, we do not even acknowledge the missing step in the sentence

> John dropped the fragile glass dish and Susan refused to sweep up the bits.

The strict validity of the inference is undoubtedly questionable, but it is the writer's responsibility that it arose.

Is the information derived from texts in fact so fickle? Are the processes of comprehension so easily seduced? To argue so presents serious difficulties, since the process seems potentially so open-ended and ungovernable. There appears to be no good reason why, having read a few sentences, the reader's own knowledge structures should not take over and supply an indefinitely large number of possible interpretations. Of course, there may be texts for which this is a desirable end – highly allusive poetry, for example – but it is not generally so. Why, after reading

> John went to a party last night. He'll be drunk again tonight.

do we limit our expectations of the reader to the belief that only one inference will be made: that John invariably gets drunk at parties? Why, in contrast, should not the reader infer 'that every time John goes to a party he meets women. Women have high voices, and high voices remind him of his mother, and thinking of his mother always makes him angry, and whenever he gets angry he gets drunk' (Clark, 1977)? What stops the reader getting locked into such an endless chain of plausible (or implausible) inference? Clark's answer to this question was to postulate a 'stop rule' which works to limit the length and nature of a chain of inference. The rule can be discussed in the context of the 'given-new' contract introduced in Chapter 5. It will be recalled that this states that for any sequence of sentences the writer must provide clues as to which information is 'old' or 'given' and which is 'new'. It is part of the contract between writer and reader that certain rules of orderly communication are followed, and written text abounds with clues to the appropriate line of inference. Clark refers to these as *bridges*.

The most straightforward bridge is that provided by a direct reference from one sentence to the next. In this case inference is restricted by the explicit indication of what is old and what is new information. For example,

My camera has a leather case. The case has a long strap.

or,

Alfred drank some whisky. The whisky made Alfred tired.

Such a writing style, characteristic of some children's readers, is stiff and soon becomes boring. The boredom can, in fact, be related to the fact that very little mental work is called for to identify new information. This bridge by means of *direct reference* can be contrasted with the *indirect reference* found in

Jane wore a red sweater. The colour suited her.

In this case there is a repetition of a reference to the same concept, but the reader is left to infer this fact, aided by the presence of the second definite article. It is a short step from indirect reference of this kind to cases where different properties of the same concept are used to establish the link from one sentence to another:

Jane wore a new sweater. The colour suited her.

or

Jane wore a new sweater. Red doesn't really suit her.

In this last example the inferential load is quite great. The reader must assume that the sentences do, in fact, cohere and don't refer to two distinct episodes, in which case it is safe to assume that both refer to the same (red) sweater. If the writer fails to live up to such expectations the reader will eventually abandon hope of making sense of what was written. The necessary 'stop rule' in all these cases is simply defined: it is that the reader must establish only the most *direct* link between the concepts employed. Thus highly probable interpretations take priority over improbable ones, and single links over more complex multiple ones.

Although Clark's 'stop rule' is helpful in drawing attention to the role played by the writer's intentions – and the reader's belief that what was written should cohere – it is not altogether satisfactory. We are left wondering whether the problem has not simply been pushed back a step. How does the reader know what the most direct inferential chain is? What determines whether an interpretation is probable or not? These, it would seem, are the fundamental questions left unanswered. A possible solution can be found by returning to the idea of script-like knowledge discussed earlier. It is likely that the reader can only securely establish one script at a time. We saw in Chapter 5 that one characteristic of human attention is that it is limited in capacity: in general, only one set of ideas is available to consciousness at any moment. This is an important regulatory mechanism. If only one script is active at a time, then inferences will be made within a single mental domain. As a result chains of inference will be limited and a definition of what constitutes a direct inferential connection can be made in terms of the properties of the script.

If readers establish one script at a time there must be fairly explicit clues in the text if and when a new script is called for. Research on this topic has scarcely begun, but at least one general observation can be made. We have discussed scripts in the context of the coding of temporal change: the movement from one state to another. Language is replete with devices for indicating the passage of time, for example, by the tense of verbs or by explicit reference to time itself (e.g. 'five hours later'). It is these references that serve as a major source of information to the reader that a new script is called for.

Part III
The skill in practice

7
Where we look when we read

Looking at things

Observe someone's eyes as they read. The movements are not
smooth, but take the form of a series of short, rapid jerks. About
four times a second they briefly come to rest, each short fixation
being followed by a rapid flick, usually from left to right (from
the reader's point of view). Figure 7.1 shows the first attempt to
record these eye movements. The reader wore a contact lens to
which was attached a very light metal pointer which touched a
paper surface covered with black smoke. The device was set up
so that each time the eye came to rest a tiny spark blew off the
sooty deposit leaving a white trace. The conclusions drawn from
this early (and somewhat heroic) study have not been substan-
tially changed by more recent research. It is clear that the eye
comes to rest several times for each line of text. Each movement
spans roughly six to eight letters. The speed of movement is very
fast. At the end of each line there is a large sweep to the start of
the next.

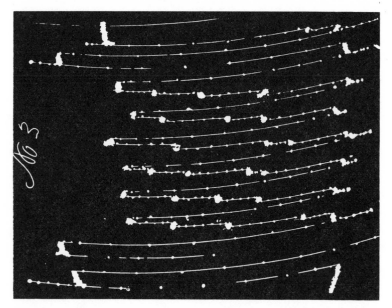

Figure 7.1 An early record of the reader's eye movements. *Source:* Huey, E. B. (1968) *The Psychology and Pedagogy of Reading*, Cambridge, Mass.: M.I.T. Press.

This jerky manner of moving the eyes is established at a very early age. Infants rapidly develop a strategy of scanning both objects and pictures in the same fashion – a series of short, jerky movements, in this case at a rate of about three a second. Figure 7.2 shows this development using a photographic recording technique. At the point where the infant is discovering what objects are, another discovery process is underway. This involves successive movement of the eyes to bring salient features such as edges and corners into central vision. Indeed, these two discovery processes are intimately linked. For the baby, learning to know *where* things are seems to be an essential first step in understanding *what* they are. The infant slowly learns to construct an inner world that represents the outside environment, and one essential component of this inner world is that it has a spatial dimension.

There is a very simple anatomical fact that makes sense of these observations. The sensitive retina of the eye is by no means

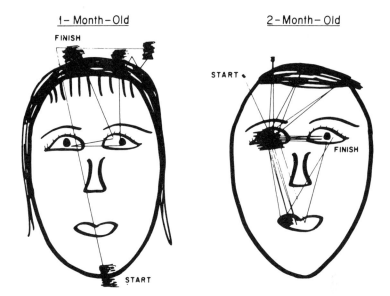

1- Month-Old   2-Month-Old

Figure 7.2 The eye movements of infants over simple line drawings. From Cohen, L. B. and Salapatek, P. (eds) (1975) *Infant Perception: from Sensation to Cognition*, New York: Academic Press.

equally good at resolving detail across the whole of its surface. In fact, resolution is only perfect in a comparatively small central region. We can demonstrate this fact to ourselves readily enough by holding the eyes steady and attempting, without eye movements, to resolve details in the visual world a little away from the centre. The ability to do this falls off very quickly as we move out into the periphery of our vision.

If we spend our time sampling the world in brief snapshots we may well ask why we are unaware of this fact. Certainly, there is a puzzling contrast here between what we know the eyes are doing and our experience of the visual world. One involves a continual change in the direction of view, the other presents us with a stable, spatially extended world to look into. It is perhaps worth bearing in mind that this inner experience is one of the end-products of a process of calculation carried out by the brain. The 'space' into which we look, and which extends to left and right, up and down, and apparently all about us, is the way the

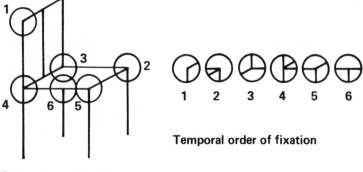

Object fixated six times

Temporal order of fixation

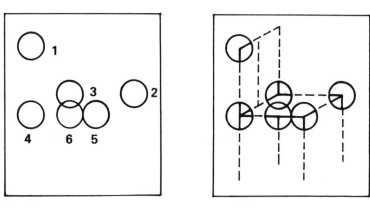

Fixations mapped into locations

Fixations assigned to locations

Figure 7.3 The relationship between the temporal order of fixations and the spatial location of their 'contents'.

brain has chosen to represent the series of discrete samples delivered to it by the eyes. In fact, the brain's solution to this problem cloaks a further paradox, since each brief image falls, as we have noted, in the *same* place on the retina; that is, each image falls on top of the one prior to it.

It may be helpful to clarify the matter with an illustration. Imagine that our only contact with the world is through a narrow tube. What we can see is restricted to a tiny segment of what is available to be inspected. We can point the tube in various directions, but when it moves no image is available. Each time it comes to rest a shutter allows us a glimpse of the world. How could we come to know what we were looking at? If we consider the case of a familiar object, such as a chair, the solution becomes evident. So long as we know – and can remember – the direction in which the tube pointed over a series of inspections the identity of the viewed object will be apparent. On the other hand, without such a record, we shall be unable to discover the nature of objects presented to us.

This example is, of course, putting an extreme case. Normally, each brief fixation delivers to the brain a complete visual field, clear at the centre and progressively more blurred towards the periphery. But the illustration captures the essence of the eye–brain problem and the manner of its solution. As the stream of fixations arrives, the brain takes account of the direction in which the eyes are pointing and places the pattern which is seen in an appropriate location in space. In this way, we are able to recognize a chair as a chair from innumerable different patterns of inspection. We do not, for example, always need to look first at the back and then at the legs. In fact, there is no 'correct' order in which features of an object must be viewed, for the simple reason that the viewer can allocate the sequence of inspections as they arrive to particular locations in an inner space (see Figure 7.3).

Looking at words

The line of print on a page is an object like any other in the sense that it has a spatially extended form. It is scanned in the same intermittent fashion as objects are scanned (see Figure 7.4). But we need to remember that printed letters represent a coded form

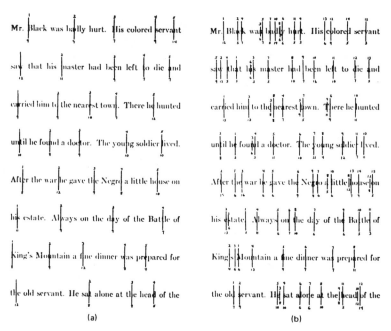

(a)　　　　　　　　　　　　　(b)

Figure 7.4 The eye movements of good and poor readers recorded using a photographic technique. *Source:* Kolers, P. A. (1976) 'Buswell's discoveries', in R. A. Monty and J. W. Senders (eds) *Eye Movements and Psychological Processes*, Hillsdale, N.J.: Erlbaum.

of speech. That is, the way the letters are arranged, their linear order, is related to another order: the temporal sequence of speech sounds. In other words, the order of the letters is of critical importance. This may appear obvious enough, but in the context of a discussion of eye movements the matter becomes a little problematic. We may consider the word as a whole to have a particular shape. In this sense it is no different from a drawing of an object and a succession of fixations can be assigned their position in space. But this is to assume that the viewer is sophisticated enough to be able to recognize the salient features of the shape. In the early stages of reading recognition of letters is itself an achievement. We can now see that an additional problem faces the beginning reader. If letters are to be assigned their sounds as a means of identifying a word, then the order in which they are treated ceases to be optional. It is still true that the object (the word as a shape) may be scanned in a variety of ways, but a special importance now attaches to the temporal order of fixations. Since the word must be spoken, some account must be taken of the order in which fixations occur. If this is not the same as their spatial order, some rearrangement will be called for. We can see in Figure 7.4 that the sequence of fixations for the child learning to read may be very complex.

If words are to be identified by means of their letters, the discriminations the reader must make are, in general, much finer than those called for in the perception of objects. For example, the written words *was* and *saw* can only be discriminated if the reader is *certain* of the order of the letters. But to know this calls for a considerable amount of mental work, since not only does the pattern perceived in a fixation have to be identified and assigned its location, but also the temporal order in which successive fixations occurred must be registered and remembered. It may be objected that this is to overstate the problem. The letters of a short word such as *was*, if fixated centrally, would all fall on the sensitive area of the retina. Why, therefore, is their order not self-evident? Why cannot it be established in a single fixation? To put the question this way is to fail to take seriously the psychological processes going on. First, the identification of letters is a considerable perceptual achievement. Second, as we saw in Figure 7.2, the 'whereness' of attributes is not something that is self-evident, it has to be worked out in a process that assigns significant segments of a pattern to particular locations in a mental space. In exactly the same way, the order in which letters occur cannot, for the novice reader, be treated as something that simply declares itself. It needs to be established by the careful direction of attention to features of the printed word, which are, essentially, its component letters.

Now, although it is *possible* to direct attention around the visual world without moving the eyes it is a most unnatural thing to do. Unnatural, because the very concept of space arose in the first place from patterns of eye movement acting as servants of attentional processes. Thus, even when a pattern *is* in central vision, if it is unfamiliar – and if the spatial order of its component parts is critical – attentional shifts will manifest themselves in small eye movements. Such patterns of inspection are to be seen in Figure 7.4. They are invariably found in the records of beginning readers. These sequences of inspection and re-inspection used to be considered as characterizing poor reading style. In fact, they show something quite different. They are a visible manifestation of the reader's attempts to sort out the order in which letters and words are disposed on the page.

Reading sequences of words

It is something of an irony that only the beginning reader is normally forced to read aloud. As fluency increases, this requirement is removed. At the same time eye movements become considerably less erratic. Apart from encounters with the occasional rare or irregular word, the identification of letter sequences ceases to demand multiple fixations. As the process of comprehension is gradually detached from the necessity to speak each word aloud there is a qualitative change in the pattern of eye movements. Large movements are made and the discrete series of inspections starts to look less effortful. Words are not invariably scanned in their correct order. There is a flexibility in patterns of inspection that resembles that found when viewing pictures. The reader, for example, may learn to skim: words may be skipped over, and in certain circumstances whole phrases receive only cursory attention (see Figures 7.5 and 7.6). That is, the reader may sample relatively little of what is on offer, and the samples may be made in quite widely separated regions.

Evidently, the fluent reader has learned to keep track of three sources of information: the content of each fixation, the order in which it arrived, and the direction of gaze. It is important to grasp that all three are needed if comprehension is to take place. This can easily be demonstrated by considering a sentence like

John kissed Mary.

Set aside for a moment the compelling, yet inadequate, belief that the words appear as they do because that is the way things are. As we have seen, this is to beg the question. If each word is fixated once only, there are six possible temporal sequences in

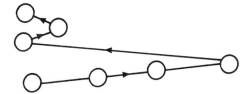

THE VEHICLE ALMOST FLATTENED A PEDESTRIAN

Figure 7.5   A sequence of eye movements over the phrase 'The vehicle almost flattened a pedestrian'. Fixations are shown as circles, their order is shown by arrows. Note that the reader concentrates attention on the first half of the sentence.

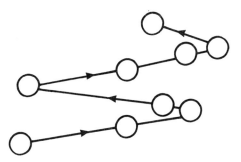

THE ARTICLE OF CLOTHING WAS MISSING

Figure 7.6   The reader spends most time on the second half.

which the contents of fixations can arrive. In terms of images within the eye all fall in more or less the same place. Clearly, some of these sequences convey inappropriate meanings (for example, 'Mary kissed John'). It is only because the reader knows the spatial (as distinct from temporal) order of the words that their correct sense can be derived.

We are forced to a rather surprising conclusion. Without conscious awareness of the fact, readers must deploy an unusual form of memory: a record of the spatial arrangement of the printed signs on the page. This spatial memory confers an advantage for the reader compared with the listener, since it allows for the possibility of re-reading what has gone before. Apart from using a very limited auditory memory, no such option is available when speech is processed. In fact, we may consider the page itself, once it has been scanned and its elements located in inner space, as a particularly powerful kind of memory. It does not fade and, so long as we know where to look, it allows for an indefinite amount of reprocessing to take place.

The control of eye movements in reading

The key question, of course, is what (if any) influences are exerted over eye movements by properties of the text being scanned? Are the eyes attracted towards significant words? Does the structure or the meaning of what is being read influence eye movements? In short, what determines where the reader looks?

Before attempting to answer these questions it is necessary to distinguish two components of the behaviour of the eyes in reading. They are not necessarily related. The first is the direction and extent of movement. It is important to grasp the fact that the mechanism controlling eye movements is *ballistic*: that is, the information that determines where the eye is to move must be available to the control process *before* a movement begins. This information might take the form of the identification of some part of the visual field needing further inspection, or it may be an internally generated command to move the eyes in a particular direction. Whatever the form of the information, once the eyes are in flight it is too late significantly to affect where they will land. While the eye is moving the visual information available is changing so rapidly that for practical purposes we may consider there to be no effective input at all. Thus, if there are aspects of text that control the direction of eye movements, and where they will land, these features must be effectively fed into the control process before the eye moves. If we consider this fact alongside what we already know of the limited powers of the eye to resolve detail away from the actual point of fixation, we can see that distinct limits will be set on the sort of text property that might influence eye movements. In fact, there is very little evidence to suggest that as readers first encounter the words of a text the meaning of what is read influences where next they look. The most potent source of influence over the size and direction of eye movements is the physical length of words lying to the right of the currently fixated word. In normal careful reading the eyes tend to move slightly to the left of the centre of the next available word. Very few eye movements fall on the spaces between words. Some small words may be passed over without being inspected at all (see Figure 7.7). In part, this may be because they are short enough to allow identification of the space that marks their conclusion. The eye may then move onto the word beyond. However, this is not a complete explanation, since there is evidence that whether a word is skipped or not depends also on its meaning. But it must be said that these word-skipping effects are relatively rare and are confined to a few, very frequent, short words (for example, the worth *the*). We may conclude that if a text is unfamiliar, or is being read for the first time, the most significant source of control over the direction and extent of eye movements is the physical length of words yet to be read.

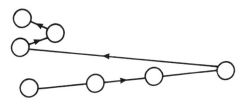

THE VEHICLE ALMOST FLATTENED A PEDESTRIAN

Figure 7.7 The word 'a' is not examined. It is likely that the word 'the' was also not looked at.

We must now consider a second important aspect of the behaviour of the eyes in reading – the duration of fixations. The question as to what factors influence the time spent inspecting words has proved very difficult to answer. This is in part because eye movements are not easy to measure and experiments on a naturally occurring effect often interfere with the process under investigation. There are, however, more serious problems. Put simply it has proved rather difficult to define exactly what a fixation is. Although we speak of the eye coming to rest, in fact it is never *absolutely* still. There are a whole series of small movements, glides and adjustments of position that make the measurement of a fixation somewhat arbitrary. Added to this difficulty is the question of what to do with the fairly frequent occurrence of several fixations on a single word (see Figure 7.4). Should these be treated as separate, or should they be collected together as a single fixation? If we adopt this latter course (which on many grounds seems sensible) several questions become unanswerable because our measure of 'fixation duration' is now no longer independent of the text. All these technical problems have held back progress towards answering an apparently simple question: does the duration of fixation relate to the meaning of what is being read?

It would be of very great assistance in the development of a theory of reading if it could be established that there are systematic variations in the time readers spend looking at the words of text. If we can demonstrate that the brain processes going on during reading influence the time spent in individual fixations, then we may turn the proposition round and use eye-movement recordings as a way of indexing the processes of comprehension. Such a subtle 'on-line' measure of reading skill would be a powerful tool for researcher and teacher alike. Unfortunately, the evidence so far available is rather unpromising. Most of the factors which are known certainly to influence the duration of a fixation are relatively uninteresting and local; that is, they do not relate to the meaning or structure of whole sentences and possibly not even to short sequences of words. A misspelling, a technical word, a word of unusual length or a rare word may produce an extended inspection, but there is little evidence that overall meaning has an effect. It would appear that the reader may move on before the processing of a particular word has been completed. What the mind is doing and where the eyes are looking are not tightly coupled together.

The argument so far may be summarized as follows. As the reader encounters words for the first time and works through a text the eyes move in a fairly regular fashion. The sources of control over these movements tend to be local physical properties of the text under inspection. In particular, a major controlling influence is the physical length of individual words. The evidence for what might be termed linguistic control is relatively slight. It is important to make this point clear, since the idea that all eye movements in reading are under direct cognitive control has been popular and is frequently proposed. The facts do not support this. Neither do they support the view that skilled readers process the meaning of words that they are not actually looking at. In fact, if they did so, the average length of an eye movement would be greater than the six or so letters usualiy found. This is not to say, of course, that fluent readers may not frequently skim through a text. But we must distinguish between being able to scan ahead because material is familiar and doing so because it is actually being processed in advance.

Looking back

So far, the discussion has been confined to eye movements over words as they are first encountered: what might be termed the first pass through the text. We have also restricted ourselves to considering normal, careful reading. However, one of the more striking properties of the eye movements of both fluent readers and beginners is the relatively large amount of time spent re-inspecting what has already been read. This is clearly evident in Figure 7.4 which shows the behaviour of children. Examples can also be found in adults (see Figure 7.8). These patterns of re-inspection have been widely misunderstood. The fact that they occur frequently in young children learning to read led some early investigators to draw the conclusion that they were a cause, rather than a result, of the child's difficulties in making sense of text. The term 'regression' was coined to capture the backward-looking nature of these inspections. This rather obscures the point, of course, that following a regression, if reading is to continue, an additional forward eye movement will be called for. What is really at issue is a place-keeping skill which depends on knowing where to look next. Nevertheless, it was concluded that regressions in some way disadvantage the child and a great deal of effort was spent in devising means for reducing their frequency. This was misguided, for two principal reasons. First, to treat regressions as an aspect of behaviour that must be eliminated prejudges the question of their possible *function*. To claim simply that they index an immature reading style is to miss the opportunity to examine precisely what purpose they may serve. Why might readers be compelled to make them? As we have seen, there is an answer to this question.

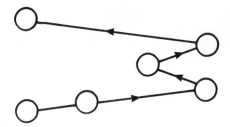

THE CRIME PREVAILED IN THE DISTRICT

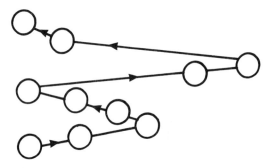

HIS RELATIVE USED A FOUNTAIN PEN

Figure 7.8   Examples of large eye movements leading to re-inspection of text already examined. (See also Figure 7.7.)

An integral part of the process of perceptual discrimination appears to involve the fine control of attention and this, in turn, has an effect on the way eye movements are distributed. It is at least possible that the re-inspections of the beginning reader reflect this effort to locate letters and words in an orderly sequence in space. The second reason is less speculative. To consider regressions merely as aberrant forms of inspection is to ignore the fact that they comprise about 10 per cent of the eye movements of even the most fluent adult reader. However skilful we become, there are always occasions when we look again at text already read. In the next section we shall attempt to deal with the question of what purpose these second looks serve.

Why look at the same word twice?

The pattern of re-inspection shown in Figure 7.8 has two important properties. First, the eye movements are quite large, sweeping across many letters. In fact, from time to time, re-inspections occur that involve moving one or more lines up the page. These large movements are comparatively infrequent, but they raise interesting questions about what information controls them. Second, an analysis of re-inspections reveals that they land in a non-random fashion. Put at its simplest, it is found that re-inspections, like other fixations, rarely fall on the spaces between words. However, in this case a greater degree of selectivity is apparent. These eye movements appear to be directed towards particular words or locations. What controls them? We have already seen that the sensitivity of the eye to detail in peripheral vision is low. Thus, it is unlikely that properties of the word to be inspected govern either the direction or extent of the movement. Not even such physical detail as a word's length, far less its meaning, would be available to the control system. Yet the movements do not have the appearance of a *search*, in which words are inspected in turn. We are left with the inescapable conclusion that readers move their eyes to particular locations because they know where words previously read are located. That is, the information that controls the movement is internally generated and not dependent on visible features of the words on the page.

It is easy to demonstrate the possibility of such internally generated control. If we close our eyes in a familiar room it is still possible to direct our line of view towards particular objects or locations. In fact, at an anecdotal level, we are all familiar with the impression or conviction that we know where on the page some sought-for information lies. The evidence suggests that these impressions are, in general, correct, even when memory over a considerable period is involved. Over shorter intervals of time readers appear to retain quite specific information, not only about what has been read, but also about where on the page particular words lie. What is being proposed here is that it is this knowledge that guides the reader's re-inspections and provides the basis for the necessary place-keeping skills that allow reading to continue smoothly following a regressive interruption.

Since some re-inspections are highly selective we may conclude that they exhibit a degree of cognitive control. The question is: how much? For what purpose does a reader, having already looked at a sequence of words, choose to look again at particular words? Is this pattern of inspection and re-inspection a *necessary* feature of skilled reading?

One approach to these very fundamental questions is to look again at the rather peculiar demands that the task of reading imposes. First, all texts can be treated as equivalent to a stream of speech. This, of course, has its own necessary order in time. However, in another sense, a text may be seen as coding a sequence of ideas and *their* chronology may be quite different. For example, in the sentence

Before John saw Mary he posted a letter.

John is mentioned before the act of posting the letter. But what the sentence declares is that the posting came first. There are similar decisions at many levels the reader must make with regard to this sentence. To make them the sequence of fixations must be used to derive a 'map' of the words in space. Thus, as we have seen, the decisions that the word *saw* (and not *was*) is present, that John saw Mary (and not vice versa), and that Mary was seen after the letter was posted, all depend on assigning the words to a unique spatial order. It is not enough to know *what* each word is (that is, the contents of each fixation), the reader must also know *where*. Once this order has been fixed, other sequences such as the order of events can be unambiguously worked out.

It is worth contrasting the demands placed on the reader with those facing the listener. Obviously, the order of speech is not an option for those who hear it, but the task of deciding on the order of events remains. The speech signal must be analysed and understood *as it arrives* or there is a serious risk that nuances of meaning – or perhaps the meaning as a whole – will be lost. For the listener there is no going back. Each ambiguity, either of word or of structure, must be dealt with by suspending decisions and holding in memory what has been said or by trying to deal simultaneously with two or more meanings. For the hearer not to lose track, what is said must be relatively unambiguous. Even so, listening imposes heavy demands on memory although we are normally unconscious of the fact. Many of these difficulties are removed for the reader. The page of text is continuously present and, once it has been scanned, it can be treated as an adjunct of the reader's memory. The code that is used to access this memory is spatial in nature – it is the knowledge the reader has derived as to where words lie. Thus ambiguity can be tolerated because the opportunity to read again is always available. The skill of reading, although undoubtedly complex and difficult to acquire, confers on fluent practitioners certain unique advantages: not the least of these is the ability to re-read at will.

The control of re-inspections

For the reader, re-inspections represent the freedom to produce alternative analyses of text. Much of this re-analysis may be restricted to sorting out the identity of individual words, but some will relate in an interesting fashion to the structure and meaning of what is being read as a whole. The main sources of control bearing on re-inspections of this kind can be related directly to the devices, discussed in Chapter 6, which produce cohesion in written material.

An obvious example is the 'given-new' contract. This, it will be recalled, allows the reader to relate sentences in an orderly fashion by making decisions about words that refer to each other. The sentences:

Jane wore a new sweater. The colour suited her.

demand that the reader make an inference. The use of the definite article in 'The colour' triggers the inference that what is referred to is the colour of the sweater. As we saw, some bridging inferences are more complex than others. The evidence suggests that as this complexity increases it takes longer to read the sentences. In fact, this increase in reading-time is used as a measure of the complexity of an inference: difficult bridges take longer to construct. But in the present context we can ask a more specific question. How do readers spend this additional time?

Do they look longer at some or all of the words? Do they look more often? Or do they do both? The answers are not entirely clear-cut, but some generalizations can be made. Longer-than-average fixations may occur, but there appears to be a limit to the amount of time readers will spend on one word – as if there were an irresistible tendency to move on after a certain time has elapsed. The bulk of the extra time is spent making more, rather than longer, fixations. Further, a significant proportion of these take the form of multiple inspections of words that refer to each other (for example, the words *colour* and *sweater* in the sentences above). The reader uses the spatial 'map' of the line of text (or indeed, the page) to direct inspections between key words.

One particularly crucial form of cross-reference in text is the use of pronouns to refer to persons or objects mentioned earlier. For example, the sentences

John stepped up to the Captain. He was holding a knife.

present the reader with a problem. To whom does the word 'He' refer: John or the Captain? Unless this can be resolved it is obvious that the meaning will be ambiguous. There are, in fact, conventions that govern the relationship between a pronoun and what it refers to. Since 'John' is the subject of the first sentence, one convention suggests that 'He' in the second sentence refers to John. Unfortunately, these rules are far from strict. If the second sentence reads,

He was holding the wheel.

pragmatic considerations might force us to conclude that 'He' refers to the Captain. The truth is that text is quite often somewhat ambiguous in this regard. Context and later sentences are used to resolve the ambiguity. Initially, the reader may be uncertain or may, in fact, make an incorrect decision. Again, the evidence suggests that in situations of this kind eye movements are directed back from the pronoun to possible candidates for cross-reference. This is not invariably found, but does occur frequently enough to demand explanation.

It is tempting, of course, to treat results of this kind as self-evident and as requiring no further explanation. After all, the facts appear straightforward: readers sometimes scan between pairs of words that refer to each other. There is, however, a puzzle. The sentences are short, and it is hard to imagine that a word is actually forgotten in a matter of seconds. Why, then, this apparently pointless process of re-examination? To answer this question we must return to the comparison of the listener's and reader's tasks. In the case of understanding speech there is only one effective method of dealing with complex cross-reference or ambiguity: various alternative interpretations must be held in memory simultaneously. The risks of adopting just one are too great, for if this turns out to be incorrect the meaning of what is being said will be lost altogether. Thus, the listener must process what is heard in great detail. Speech, as a means of communication, is replete with devices for easing this task. Intonation and stress can be used to signal the appropriate resolution of possible ambiguity. In addition, there are a variety of non-verbal signals that serve the same purpose. Above all, the speaker (unlike the writer) is able to monitor the progress of communication and take steps to limit the density of information being conveyed. There is a very clear upper limit on what can be said and understood. In contrast, the reader is able to suspend decisions about meaning or structure until enough information becomes available to arrive at a single, coherent representation. The first pass through a text need only result in a single, superficial interpretation. A particular word, for example, need only be processed to a level of unambiguous representation. Beyond this, all the reader need know is its location. When the text demands further processing (for example, bridging inferences) the reader can always look back. Looking again at the word is the most effective way of accessing again the mental lexicon.

This is a radical proposal. It suggests that the reader is released from many of the obligations imposed on the hearer. Whereas speech, once heard, is lost forever, written text remains continuously available and the fact that it is spatially coded allows the reader rapid and flexible access to it. Of course, for a straightforward text a relatively superficial analysis will be enough to arrive at its meaning. But this initial interpretation incurs little cost since, if the reader encounters unexpected complexities or ambiguity, selective re-inspection can be used to repair the fault.

Eye movements, therefore, carry a dual function. Obviously, they are employed as the primary means of presenting text for visual processing. However, in addition, they are brought into the service of the spatially coded representation which the reader forms. These two aspects can be related to what we have termed the two passes through the text. The first pass (which may be the only one made) is used to derive a single, unambiguous representation of meaning. It may be looked on as relatively passive in the sense that printed words, in turn, are used to access the mental lexicon. In addition, the reader allocates the printed symbols to unique locations in a mental space. This spatial 'map' is retained in memory in enough detail to allow for the identification of some or all words on the page. The second pass involves more active processes. Faulty interpretations are corrected, points of cross-reference are established, and ambiguities resolved. In all these activities the spatially coded memory is used to guide selective re-inspections of the printed page.

The necessity of looking back

The theory outlined in the previous section is somewhat contentious. In this section some evidence in support of it will be set out. This will take the form of three illustrations. In the first, we shall consider what happens when readers are deliberately confronted with systematic ambiguity in text. In the second, evidence will be presented that suggests that readers make use of spatially coded information even when their eye movements do *not* produce any visual input. From this rather artificial situation we are led to ask a crucial question. What is the consequence of denying to a reader the possibility of establishing a unique spatial map of the page? In other words, to what extent are re-inspections actually *necessary* for comprehension? The third illustration looks at a reading situation where re-inspections cannot occur.

In Chapter 5 the point was made that sentences that are structurally ambiguous simply should not occur in normal text. To produce them is to break the implicit contract between writer and reader. Although this is so, the observation obscures the fact that many sentences are *in part* inescapably ambiguous. That is, they are capable of more than one interpretation up to a particular point, beyond which only one meaning becomes possible. Such *temporary* ambiguity is quite common. For example, the sentence

While the teacher was reading the book fell off the table.

can easily be initially misunderstood. One is tempted to construct a meaning for 'While the teacher was reading the book', and then encounter difficulty dealing with the rest of the sentence. The word 'fell' can be treated as critical in the interpretation of the sentence. It acts to resolve the ambiguity. One way of looking at such a sentence is to treat the phrase 'was reading the book' as being capable of two interpretations. The theory outlined in the last section suggests that readers will not, in fact, do this. The evidence from eye-movement recordings, at least in part, supports this interpretation. Fluent adult readers tend to reach the key disambiguating word and then pause or make one or more selective re-inspections. A typical movement of this kind for the sentence quoted above would be from the word 'fell' to the word 'teacher'. It would be wrong to suggest that such re-inspections *always* occur, but they are frequent enough to provide some support for the idea that selective re-inspection is used to correct an inappropriate interpretation.

The second line of evidence is derived from a somewhat unusual reading situation. The text to be read took the form of quite difficult verbal problems. For example:

All taxis are cars. Some cars are unsafe. (Some taxis are unsafe.)

The reader's task was to decide whether the statement in brackets followed from the two initial sentences. The two initial sentences were presented on a display screen and could be examined at length. Sometimes they were scanned back and forth for up to ten seconds – that is, time to look at each word five or more times (see Figure 7.9). It would appear that as readers attempt to understand these sentences (and possibly construct a mental model to represent their meaning), it is of help to direct attention repeatedly towards relevant words. Obviously, since the sentences are so short, an alternative strategy would have

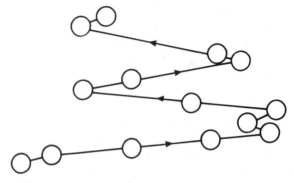

ALL MEN ARE MORTAL.   SOCRATES IS A MAN.

Figure 7.9   Typical patterns of inspection over the two premises of a syllogism. Note the multiple re-inspections.

been to memorize them and then operate on a verbal code. Such a strategy would be the only one available to someone who simply heard the two sentences. However, readers choose not to do this, and again we have quite striking evidence of the apparently close coupling between attention and direction of gaze.

Once the sentences had been read, the display screen became blank and the final statement (placed in brackets above) was presented *auditorily*. As this was being assessed a record was taken (unknown to the readers) of any eye movements directed towards the blank display screen. Some typical records are shown in Figure 7.10. Quite clearly, as readers work out the solution to these problems, non-random eye movements occur. The locations inspected yield no useful visual information but they are made, presumably, because a word and its location have become closely linked together.

The fact that eye movements of this kind occur does not, of course, establish that they are *necessary*. To examine this proposition we must turn to the third piece of evidence. It is possible to present text to a reader in a way that does not call for individual eye movements at all. To do this each word must be presented in a single location for an appropriate period. The reader need do no more than fixate this location and process the words of text as they appear. Although the situation is a little artificial it will be

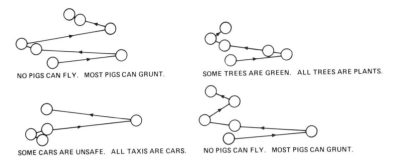

NO PIGS CAN FLY. MOST PIGS CAN GRUNT.   SOME TREES ARE GREEN. ALL TREES ARE PLANTS.

SOME CARS ARE UNSAFE. ALL TAXIS ARE CARS.   NO PIGS CAN FLY. MOST PIGS CAN GRUNT.

Figure 7.10 Eye movements over the locations previously occupied by the sentences illustrated. The words were not present when the recordings were made.

appreciated that in many respects the conditions of normal reading are adequately reproduced. Each word falls in central vision and is replaced by the next after an appropriate interval. All that is missing is the requirement to move the eyes. There is one simple way of ensuring that the duration of each fixation is adequate: that is to place the display under the control of the reader. For example, each word can be displayed as a button is pressed. Text can thus be processed word by word at a pace to suit the reader. There is, however, no possibility of looking back in this situation.

What is predicted? Clearly any text that leads the reader to an inappropriate initial interpretation will now present serious problems. If the reader is unable to back up and carry out a re-analysis we would expect comprehension to be impaired. Obviously, temporary ambiguities of the kind discussed earlier in this section represent appropriate material to test this prediction. The results, in general, support the theory. When ambiguous sentences of this kind are presented word by word in the same location they prove difficult to understand.

8
Failure
and
success

Dyslexia

Reading is such a complicated skill it is virtually impossible to study it in the normal fluent adult. Whatever the numerous component processes may be, they are so effortlessly deployed that they are quite transparent to the observer. True, as psychologists we can attempt to abstract plausible component skills (for example, the ability to recognize and pronounce words) and observe their operation in an experimental context, but there is little or no evidence to be had from the normal reader in a normal environment. Reading is a solitary affair, involving one person and a book. Its end-product cannot be measured directly since it is a purely mental event – a state of knowledge. It follows that there is a suspicion among teachers and others concerned with reading in practice that attempts by psychologists to analyse the component processes are artificial, unrealistically abstract and, in general, unhelpful. This impatience is easy to understand but is not altogether justified. The first seven chapters of this book have provided a number of arguments that there exist sub-skills in reading. In this section we shall be considering one further category of evidence: the study of particular forms of brain damage. When this occurs in some people they become dyslexic, that is they may, to varying degrees, be unable to read. Fortunately this symptom is fairly rare, but its occurrence is of particular interest to the psychologist since we can learn a great deal about a process from studying the way in which it breaks down. Such insights are invaluable since they give us confidence that the mental processes that we have suggested underlie reading skill have some kind of reality. It is important to get clear the point of this exercise. It is not being suggested that reading failure is invariably caused by brain damage: this would be a ludicrous proposal. However, brain damage does, sometimes, produce unique disorders of reading. We can use such cases to improve our understanding of how the intact brain treats the process. That is, how component processes are partitioned out by the brain. When we know this, we shall have a better grasp on which aspects of reading it is reasonable to treat as having functional independence.

When the brain is injured, by a blow for example, or as a result of a stroke, the effects produced depend very much on *where* the injury takes place. Some mental functions, in particular those relating to the use of language, are carried out in distinct regions of the brain. When such a region is damaged the relevant function can be impaired while other skills remain relatively unaffected. Some of the processes relating to reading appear to be of this kind. If we can be convinced of this, we may conclude that the relevant mental operations are, to some degree, genuinely independent. Such a conclusion would be, of course, of enormous practical consequence, since it would influence the manner in which reading is taught.

Although there is great variation in the symptoms displayed, brain-damaged people who have lost the ability to read fluently typically fall into one or another of two broad categories. The first is characterized by a patient trying to read, but finding great difficulty in understanding. Reading aloud is particularly difficult, although the problem is not related simply to a speech disorder since such patients may have no problems holding a conversation. In other words, their disorder appears to be quite specific: it relates to producing the sounds of written words. The difficulty such patients find appears to arise from the fact that they have only one way of dealing with text; namely, to translate it to sound. But, as we have discovered, such a method can be successful only in a very limited sense, since the rules that relate letters to sounds have many exceptions. It is perhaps more profitable to ask what it is that such patients *cannot* do. The answer is quite clear: they have no way of using the *visual form* of written words to arrive at their meaning. They are, in a sense, forced to rely on a strategy normally only dominant in the earliest stages of learning to read. However, for such patients the problem is made more severe because they do not have, and find it virtually impossible to acquire, the ability to recognize even common words by the way they look.

It will hardly have escaped notice that this form of reading failure is consistent with the description we gave in Chapter 4 (see Figures 4.1 and 4.2) of the two routes to meaning. These clinical observations *could* be taken to suggest rather strongly that brain damage may lead to the selective impairment of one route. However, to clinch such an argument we need first to find another category of patient with the opposite pattern of disability; that is, able to read words but unable to employ letter-to-sound rules to pronounce them. This is not, of course, a contradiction. In terms of the psychological theory illustrated in Figure 4.3 it is perfectly possible for someone to know how to pronounce a word and yet at the same time be unable to translate its printed form into an appropriate sequence of sounds.

In fact, patients of this kind exist and have been the subject of many psychological studies. The nature of their disability may not at first be obvious since they can often read words quite fluently. They are not, however, using letter-to-sound rules. This becomes obvious if such patients are presented with a non-word which is, nevertheless, perfectly pronounceable. The string of letters 'strondle', for example, poses an insuperable problem for such patients. Since 'strondle' is not a word (that is, cannot be recognized by its form) they have no resources to deal with it. It is correct to describe such patients as dyslexic since, although they can recognize words by their visual form, they are quite unable to use the *sound* of letters to achieve the same result. Their injury has denied them the use of spelling-to-sound rules. We may ask, of course, how in that case they come to be able to read aloud at all. But the answer here follows clearly from the theory presented in Chapter 4. Reading aloud involves rules for the production of speech that are quite distinct from the letter-to-sound rules a reader may come to discover after a great deal of experience with print. We can speak long before we can read.

Are we justified, then, in treating this clinical evidence as conclusive support for the notion that reading does, in fact, involve at least two component processes which are capable of acting independently? If such a proposal could be established beyond doubt it would be an important intellectual advance since it would license certain practices in teaching and in the remedial treatment of poor readers. We might, for example, feel justified in concentrating on one 'sub-process' to the exclusion of others if we believe that such distinct components of the overall skill are capable of acting independently. It is just such a conclusion that the study of brain-damaged patients appears to invite. It is difficult, however, to accept the proposition without qualification. The reason for hesitation will become more clear when we attempt to relate what we know of the reading performance of brain-damaged patients to that of normal people without brain damage, who nevertheless have trouble learning to read.

The fact that injury can cause *selective* impairment in reading skill is impressive, but we should be cautious in jumping to conclusions. Patients with brain damage often have other communication problems of a rather general kind. They may not, in fact, be able to *read* at all in the sense that the term has been defined in this book. Dealing with individual words in isolation is only a small part of the repertoire of a fluent reader. If it represents *all* that someone can manage, we may be inclined to deny that such a person can read. The danger is that we may seize on those aspects of the behaviour of brain-damaged patients that appear to support, or are at least consistent with, our theories and neglect, or ignore, equally reliable findings that are inconsistent. Patients often show symptoms that cannot easily be accommodated by *any* particular psychological theory. For example, brain damage can result in a reader having more difficulty with words that refer to abstract concepts, like 'pride' and 'honesty', than with words that refer to real, tangible objects, like 'table' and 'knife'. Similarly, it is quite often found, following brain damage, that nouns are read more easily than other parts of speech. These observations cannot be explained by anything obvious such as the relative familiarity of the words used. In fact, there is no satisfactory account of *why* such effects should occur. We are simply left with an uncomfortable intuition that the apparent 'reading difficulty' is, in reality, just one manifestation of a much more complex and diffuse pattern of disorder affecting a whole range of mental activities. Once this possibility is opened up we are forced to examine again what might be cause and what effect. Reading is a communicative endeavour involving a lot of subtle inferential processes on the part of the practitioner. From this point of view we may see mental sub-processes, not as masters, but as servants of some other function of which we have a far less certain psychological understanding.

So far, we have confined the use of the term dyslexia to cases of reading impairment induced by brain damage. It may, however, be applied to people with no known brain damage who experience exceptional difficulty with reading. It is important in such cases to rule out other possible causes of failure such as poor school attendance, low motivation, or an adverse social environment. A child who reads no better than someone two or more years younger and yet is otherwise of normal intelligence and has no particular environmental or social handicap is often said to be suffering from *developmental dyslexia*. Two things need to be said about this term. First, it is a relatively unhelpful label. In one sense, of course, it does no more than redescribe the child's problem and might be judged innocent enough. But the difficulty goes a little deeper. The term suggests a particular physical disorder: indeed, hinting at the very thing that the definition expressly excludes, namely brain damage. In this light, such a definition does little to help and may even do harm, since it implies that the fault, whatever it may be, lies beyond remedy; and that may not be true. It is, in fact, a double-edged misconception. In the first place, a disability caused by brain damage is not, thereby, necessarily permanent. It is perfectly possible to recover functions that have been lost and to relearn old skills. In the second place, all human activities show individual differences. It is true, therefore, but totally empty, to ascribe such variation to differences in brain function. Thus, if I am not very good at playing the piano or doing crosswords I might claim that the incapacity was a result of the way my brain is constructed. But quite obviously this is not a very illuminating proposal. It answers no questions and leads to no conclusions. We shall, therefore, in the following two sections, look at reading failure in the context of purely psychological issues. No attempt will be made to define 'the dyslexic person', since it is highly unlikely that straightforward causes can be isolated. It is, nevertheless, important to look at the range of individual differences and at those aspects of reading that appear to be most vulnerable.

Perceptual problems

An obvious starting point when looking at variations in proficiency is to examine the purely perceptual demands posed by reading and to try to identify which, if any, give rise to particular problems for the learner. The early stages of reading call for the development of some highly unusual skills. A reader must learn what, in visual terms, defines a letter. That is, which of the innumerable pieces of evidence available on the page serve to distinguish one letter from all others. Readers must also become aware of certain properties of spoken language: to the degree that letters come to be accepted as referring to the idea of a particular kind of sound. Both these skills involve isolating relevant events in a welter of irrelevant information. The mental work involved in this perceptual learning is very great: it is worth asking whether individuals differ in their ability to carry it out.

Fortunately, the answers are reasonably clear-cut. There are differences in both the speed and accuracy with which different individuals can isolate and recognize visual forms. However, this variability between people is not a particularly potent cause of reading failure. Good readers and poor readers do not systematically differ in their ability to process visual forms. In contrast, when we come to examine individual variation in the processing of *sounds* we find a very different picture. Poor readers are quite strikingly slower and less accurate in making use of segments of speech to gain access to the meaning of words. Some backward readers appear to find the task difficult largely because they cannot efficiently use the 'indirect' route to meaning shown in Figure 4.1. It is important to grasp that such a problem will have cumulative effects for the learner. The rules of letter-to-sound correspondence are of particular use in dealing with new words. Visual aspects of a word are of little help to someone with only limited experience of print. True, the purely visual route to meaning does come eventually to be dominant. But in the early stages the reader must make extensive use of letter-to-sound rules. The reward for success in this venture is an increasing degree of independence. The penalty for failure is a frustrating dependence on some other person to identify new words.

We have already seen, in brain-damaged patients, that this particular skill in dealing with letters as coded sounds can be selectively impaired. We are now left asking why, in a person without brain damage, the same ability may be affected. It is tempting, of course, to propose that, for some unknown reason, the component skill has been 'damaged' or become ineffective. But if we take this way out there is little left to be said: the failing reader is seen as analogous to the brain-damaged patient, but with the qualification that no brain damage is present. Quite obviously this is unsatisfactory. Perhaps we should resist the apparent similarities and look for an alternative answer. One such can be found by stepping back and considering the purpose of learning to read. To become proficient, or even to get started, it is essential to know what the business is about: that reading is a way of arriving at ideas by looking at print. It is an activity concerned with *meaning*. Without this insight many of the activities that engage the child early on in learning to read may appear unrewardingly arbitrary. The results shown in Figure 3.6, for example, neatly illustrate that distinctions made by the teacher must be seen, not as self-evident facts, but as part of the teacher's repertoire of concepts. Eventually these must become part of the child's knowledge, but before this can happen an appropriate way of discussing the enterprise as a whole must be discovered. To learn to read the child must find a way of becoming aware of some of its own mental processes. This aspect of the task – the need to stand outside the activity and reflect on its purpose – can easily be neglected. If it is, the fact that teacher and pupil must traffic in concepts and not in self-evident properties of the world will become an immediate and major obstacle.

It was proposed in Chapter 3 that the way we understand things (and in the context of learning to read, it is the sounds of speech and the shapes of letters and words that are important) is constrained by the theories we hold about them. Only when we have a secure grasp of a concept can we tolerate an abstract representation of it. Now this notion has very lively consequences if it is seriously applied to the process of learning to read. Many of the critical distinctions in speech are difficult to recover from the pattern of sound striking the ear. In learning to speak and understand speech, we discover what these essential properties are. But this hard-won knowledge is not itself readily described. Much as we are unable to say what it is we 'know' when we have learned to swim or to ride a bicycle, we may be unable to articulate what we have discovered in learning to speak. Being able to describe one's own mental life involves both a degree of insight and, above all, an appropriate vocabulary. For example, it is pointless to attempt to show the similarity in a family of words such as 'pat', 'bat', 'sat' and 'cat' to a child who has so far failed to become aware of rhyme. To our sophisticated ears, of course, the common sound is self-evident. What we are inclined to forget is that it is, in fact, an abstraction (one of many possible) drawn from the set of sounds defining the four words in question.

Since this whole argument could easily be judged as overstated, an illustration may clarify matters. Skilled wine-tasters (or tea-tasters for that matter) are often held up to ridicule. The reason is that most of us cannot taste what they claim to be self-evident. Hence, we all enjoy stories of some dreadful lapse in which inferior wine is misclassified as being of great quality. But the truth is that experienced wine-tasters really *can* discriminate between wines that, to the novice, appear identical in taste. The fact that wine-tasters then attempt to convey the distinctions they make, using florid descriptive terms such as 'bold' or 'young', only seems to make matters worse. For most of us, the distinctions to which these 'theoretical terms' refer are simply not there to be made. It is salutary to reflect on the fact that the beginning reader is faced with an entirely analogous situation. Readers differ in their ability to grasp the terms that must be used if the relationships between letter and sound are to be learned. The consequences for those who fail in this are severe since, without special attention, a reader may fall so far behind that the task as a whole becomes both overwhelmingly difficult and meaningless.

Eye movements

It is perhaps appropriate at this point to examine one of the most persistent hypotheses with regard to reading failure. It has been known for almost a century that the pattern of eye movements in good and poor readers differs. The person in difficulty is easy to spot: there are many more eye movements to each line, more re-inspections within a word, and more re-inspections of words on a line of text. Not surprisingly, observations such as these led many early investigators to conclude that poor eye-movement control was a major cause of failure to read. The remedy seemed equally clear. If, by means of a programme of training, the reader could be induced to modify these habits – that is, to make fewer inspections, fewer re-inspections, fewer backward eye movements, and so on – then reading should improve. This is a plausible enough idea and gains some support from the fact that poor control over the muscles of the eyes would certainly lead to difficulties in word recognition. As we have seen, being able to locate letters in a spatial order depends on knowledge about where the eyes are pointing. If this information is, for any reason, less than perfect, difficulties will clearly ensue.

However appealing this line of argument might seem, we should view it with great suspicion. Poor eye-movement control would undoubtedly lead to problems with reading, but quite obviously it would lead to other, far more grave, difficulties in addition. The identification of objects would be impaired, as would the recognition of pictures. There is no evidence that reading failure as it is normally found goes hand-in-hand with such disabilities. In fact, as we have already noted, perceptual problems affecting visual processing do not seem to be characteristic of reading failure at all. We must conclude that the patterns of eye movements found in the poor reader are much more likely to relate to attempts to make sense of text. In other words, we must face again a tendency to confuse cause and effect. The poor reader's erratic eye movements are a *result*, and not a cause, of reading difficulty. We may recall from Chapter 7 that the eye movements characteristic of the second pass through a text serve to link elements of meaning together. Difficulty in making sense of text at this level will, therefore, quite naturally lead to erratic patterns of inspection. (We should note in passing that the reader who becomes dependent on the first pass through text may derive only a relatively impoverished representation of it's meaning.)

Efforts to train eye movements in reading are therefore bound to be unsuccessful. The source of control over first pass eye movements is simply not accessible to consciousness. To exercise effective control by means of a programme of training would involve allowing the reader some way of knowing at each point in a text where next to look. But, as we have seen, the information from any particular fixation could never be consciously available in time to influence the next. Such a training programme would, therefore, be doomed. Attempting to treat reading disability by changing eye movements is rather like attempting to alter the weather by adjusting a barometer. It is absurd to direct remedial efforts towards the results rather than the causes of failure.

Cognitive problems

So far, we can summarize the problems of the failing reader by noting that the most potent difficulty is coming to see writing as a form of coded speech. This problem is far more common than any perceptual difficulty in recognizing words by their visual form. There are, however, other sources of difficulty with which the reader must contend. These relate to cognitive aspects of the task.

We defined the goal of reading as establishing a representation of meaning. To arrive at this involves more than merely identifying the words on the page: what must be achieved is an understanding of whole sequences of sentences. The reader must identify the writer's intention: a contract must be established. Chapters 5 and 6 dealt in detail with the mechanics of this process; in particular, the identification of clues in a text that reveal given and new information and allow the reader to share some of the writer's presuppositions. While the complexity of these operations obviously varies, they are as necessary for the beginner as for the fluent adult. Enough information must be gained from the printed page to permit the construction of a mental representation of what is written. This invariably involves processes of inference that go well beyond the literal meaning of words on the page. In the early stages of learning to read, such a process can be seen as having both advantages and disadvantages. For the reader 'in the know' much of what is unsaid will be silently and effortlessly conveyed. Faced with the same text, the failing reader will meet gaps and uninterpretable signals. The text will fail to cohere, no contract will be established with the writer, and the meaning as a whole of what is written will not become established in the reader's mind.

If we glance again at Figure 4.3 it will be appreciated why such a situation produces such grave problems. Unless a pattern of focused activity can be established in the mental lexicon, context cannot play its appropriate regulatory role. Ambiguity will be discovered where, for the more practised reader, none exists. Points of cross-reference will not be established. The ability to predict what comes next will be diminished, with a consequential increase in the mental work needed to identify words. In short, the two-way relationship between the reader's knowledge and the processes of word identification will fail to function.

All these problems characterize the reader in difficulty. Why should they arise? The answer again appears to be that initial failure is likely to trap the beginner in a cycle of difficulty. Context becomes, broadly speaking, of *less* help to poorer readers. This is something of a surprise since we might expect the person in difficulty to guess more often. But the psychological evidence suggests that to make effective use of context (for example, to identify a new word) a reader must be at least moderately skilful. It is the poor reader who becomes tied to the text: the task of word identification demanding so much attention that the overall purpose of the exercise becomes lost. Reading aloud makes matters worse, since it is difficult to give a sentence as a whole its proper intonation and phrasing if the words are separated by long pauses. Thus, even if all words are correctly identified, the sentence as a whole will not sound remotely like the same sentence produced in the child's spontaneous speech. It is all too easy in such a situation to arrive at incorrect beliefs about the nature of reading. For the beginner, continual support must be provided for the proposition that print can be used to activate knowledge. That is, words are not *merely* coded sounds. Unless this is achieved it is rather unlikely that texts will be recognized for what they are – coherent representations of meaning. The failing reader finds it particularly difficult to integrate and make automatic the numerous skills that underpin the task. As a result, words may well be identified, but their *value* – in terms of the meaning of a text – be ignored. Thus, an activity that should serve to liberate the mind may rapidly come to be seen as essentially pointless and sterile.

To emphasize in this way the reader's knowledge and beliefs about the nature of reading is not, of course, to deny the importance of being able to recognize and identify individual letters and words. It is, however, necessary to place these skills in an appropriate perspective. After many years of psychological investigation, it remains true that there are few, if any, important differences between successful and failing readers in what might be termed the component processes of reading. The problems appear to arise elsewhere. First, it is necessary for the child to grasp the mysterious fact that significant aspects of spoken language are captured in written forms. This awareness is an essential liberating step that allows us, unaided, to arrive at the meaning of new words. Second, reading must be recognized for what it is: a form of communication. The meaning that is arrived at becomes, of course, part of the reader's mental life: it is not a message that can be extracted from print. To understand involves a leap beyond what is written to share some of the writer's concepts.

Although reading failure *can* be discussed in terms of the malfunction of some component process – as if a part in a machine had failed – we ought to remind ourselves that in doing so we are using a metaphor. The function of the human mind is not well illustrated by such comparisons since its 'components' seem to be so completely interdependent. An overwhelming tendency of mental life is to find order and meaning in the environment. This tendency is so strong that it is hard to escape the conclusion that some very great evolutionary advantage was secured for *homo sapiens* in this way. From this point of view, reading takes its place, not as some exotic admixture of sub-skills precariously held together, but as one among many ways of finding meaning 'out there'.

Coming to read

We have dwelt on failure and its causes, but it is reasonable to ask what psychology can say about success at reading. Clearly, there is much that could be said on the question of *learning* to read and psychological expertise has greatly influenced the practices of teachers. But this is not a book about the techniques of teaching and these final comments will, therefore, be some-what general.

The vital step for the learner is to discover a way of becoming *independent*. That is, a way of tackling text without continual recourse to some other person to decypher particular words. So far as is known, there is really only one way in which this can be achieved, at least initially. This is to become aware of corre-spondences between letter forms and sounds. To gain such knowledge the reader must solve two problems: the effortless recognition of letter sequences, and some insight into the nature of the components of speech. This last point is of necessity vague, for we do not yet know how deep this insight must be. What is undeniable is that the reader must somehow be placed in a position where aspects of spoken language can be discussed in a meaningful way. Until this knowledge can be shared between teacher and pupil little progress will occur.

Once the reader is independent, however, new routes to meaning can be employed. In particular, increasing fluency is marked by increasing use of the visual form of a word to gain immediate access to its meaning. Once a text is seen as being meaningful as a whole the reader may rely on context to support the identification of words. A process of very sophisticated guessing begins. Initially, the identification of words is an all-consuming activity, but gradually this becomes secondary to the development of a representation of meaning. The key to this transition is a recognition that written text is not, in fact, a code to be decyphered, but a rather elaborate means of communication. It is crucial here that the beginner understands how great are the similarities between the tasks of writer and reader and those of speaker and listener. Both demand similar mental processes, both make similar assumptions. In particular, and above all, the reader must believe that text makes sense and has a purpose. This means coming to a belief that as readers we have a contract with the writer; it is likely that encounters in the role of hearer are as important in this regard as those in the role of reader. The key element in such exchanges is the gradual emergence of a form of language that stands apart from and comments on language itself. When teacher and pupil have a repertoire of terms that point to a common knowledge of such things as rhyme, stress and segmentation, it is relatively straightforward to bring this to bear on the 'derived' skill of reading.

The more the reader knows, the less work the text has to do. Knowledge is thus not an adjunct for the learner (something that the text mysteriously conveys), but an essential and cardinal prerequisite for understanding. In this sense reading is unlike arithmetic or geometry which exist in their own, highly circum-scribed domains. Texts are allusive – they convey variable amounts of information – it is for the reader to do the necessary mental work. The belief that words have merely to be decoded to arrive at sense must be abandoned as misleading and fundamentally incorrect.

Reading is a human activity and it rests on the assumption that human communication is going on. The depiction of meaning, with which we began this book, is a ubiquitous activity. We all, at some time, seek to capture meaning in pictorial form. Reading – even of an alphabetic script – represents a continuation of this ancient process.

References

Clark, H. H. (1977) 'Bridging' in P. N. Johnson-Laird and P. C. Wason (eds) *Thinking*, Cambridge: Cambridge University Press.

Collins, A. M. and Quillian, M. R. (1972) 'How to make a language user' in E. Tulving and W. Donaldson (eds) *Organisation of Memory*, New York: Academic Press.

Gibson, E. J. and Levin, H. (1975) *The Psychology of Reading*, Cambridge, Mass.: M.I.T. Press.

Gombrich, E. H. J. (1965) *Meditation on a Hobby Horse and other Essays on the Theory of Art*, London: Phaidon.

Gombrich, E. H. J. (1982) *The Image and the Eye. Further Studies in the Psychology of Pictorial Representation*, London: Phaidon.

Grice, H. P. (1975) 'Logic and conversation' William James Lectures, Harvard University Press, 1967. In P. Cole and J. L. Morgan (eds) *Studies in Syntax, III*, New York: Academic Press.

Haviland, S. E. and Clark, H. H. (1974) 'What's new? Acquiring new information as a process in comprehension', *Journal of Verbal Learning and Verbal Behavior*, 13, 512–21.

Huey, E. B. (1908) *The Psychology and Pedagogy of Reading*, reprinted 1968, Cambridge, Mass.: M.I.T. Press.

Katz, J. J. and Fodor, J. A. (1963) 'The structure of a semantic theory', *Language*, 39, 170–210.

Kintsch, W. and Monk, D. (1972) 'Storage of information in memory: some implications of the speed with which inferences can be made', *Journal of Experimental Psychology*, 94, 25–32.

Ladefoged, P. and Broadbent, D. E. (1957) 'Information conveyed by vowels', *Journal of the Acoustical Society of America*, 29, 98–104.

Levelt, W. J. M. (1969) 'The perception of syntactic structure', Invited paper to the XIX International Congress of Psychology, London, July 27–August 2.

Lisker, L. and Abramson, A. (1970) 'The voicing dimension: some experiments in comparative phonetics', *Proceedings of Sixth International Congress of Phonetic Sciences, Prague, 1967*, Prague: Academia.

Pichert, J. W. and Anderson, R. C. (1977), 'Taking different perspectives on a story', *Journal of Educational Psychology*, 69, 309–15.

Schank, R. C. (1975) 'The role of memory in language processing' in C. N. Cofer (ed.) *The Structure of Human Memory*, San Francisco: Freeman.

Taylor, I. (1899) *The Alphabet*, I–II, London: Edward Arnold.

Additional reading

Chapter 1

Frith, U. (1980) *Cognitive Processes in Spelling*, London: Academic Press.

Gregory, R. L. (1970) *The Intelligent Eye*, London: Weidenfeld and Nicolson.

Henderson, L. (1982) *Orthography and Word Recognition in Reading*, London: Academic Press.

Henderson, L. (ed.) (1984) *Orthographies and Reading*, Hillsdale, N.J.: Erlbaum.

Huey, E. B. (1908) *The Psychology and Pedagogy of Reading*, reprinted 1968, Cambridge, Mass.: M.I.T. Press.

Chapter 2

Johnson-Laird, P. N. and Wason, P. C. (eds) (1977) *Thinking*, Cambridge: Cambridge University Press.

Neisser, U. (1967) *Cognitive Psychology*, New York: Appleton-Century-Crofts.

Neisser, U. (1976) *Cognition and Reality*, San Francisco: Freeman.

O'Connor, J. D. (1976) *Phonetics*, London: Pelican Books.

Reynolds, A. G. and Flagg, P. (1983) *Cognitive Psychology* (2nd edition), Boston, Mass.: Little, Brown and Company.

Chapter 3

Aitchison, J. (1976) *The Articulate Mammal*, London: Hutchinson.

Gibson, E. J. and Levin, H. (1975) *The Psychology of Reading*, Cambridge, Mass.: M.I.T. Press.

Greene, J. (1972) *Psycholinguistics*, Harmondsworth: Penguin.

Kavanagh, J. F. and Mattingly, I. G. (1972) *Language by Ear and by Eye*, Cambridge, Mass.: M.I.T. Press.

Singer, C. (1959) *A Short History of Scientific Ideas*, Oxford: Oxford University Press.

Chapter 4

Anderson, J. R. (1980) *Cognitive Psychology and its Implications*, San Francisco: Freeman.

Clark, H. H. and Clark, E. V. (1977) *Psychology and Language: an Introduction to Psycholinguistics*, New York: Harcourt Brace Jovanovich.

Fodor, J. A., Bever, T. G. and Garrett, M. F. (1974) *The Psychology of Language*, New York: McGraw-Hill.

Levin, H. and Williams, J. P. (eds) (1970) *Basic Studies on Reading*, New York: Basic Books.

Mitchell, D. C. (1982) *The Process of Reading*, London: Wiley.

Chapter 5

Bobrow, D. G. and Collins, A. (eds) (1975) *Representation and Understanding*, New York: Academic Press.

Kintsch, W. (1977) *Memory and Cognition*, New York: Wiley.

Lyons, J. (ed.) (1970) *New Horizons in Linguistics*, Baltimore: Penguin.

Norman, D. A. (ed.) (1970) *Models of Human Memory*, New York: Academic Press.

Chapter 6

Johnson-Laird, P. N. and Wason, P.C. (1977) *Thinking*, Cambridge: Cambridge University Press.

Lakoff, G. (1980) *Metaphors We Live By*, Chicago: Chicago University Press.

Levinson, S. C. (1983) *Pragmatics,* Cambridge: Cambridge University Press.

Sanford, A. J. and Garrod, S. C. (1981) *Understanding Written Language,* London: Wiley.

Schank, R. C. and Abelson, R. (1977) *Scripts, Plans, Goals and Understanding: an Enquiry into Human Knowledge Structures,* Hillsdale, N.J.: Erlbaum.

Schank, R. C. (1982) *Dynamic Memory: a Theory of Reminding and Learning in Computers and People,* Cambridge: Cambridge University Press.

Werth, P. (ed.) (1981) *Conversation and Discourse,* London: Croom Helm.

Chapter 7

Monty, R. A. and Senders, J. W. (1976) *Eye Movements and Psychological Processes,* Hillsdale, N.J.: Erlbaum.

Rayner, K. (ed.) (1983) *Eye Movements in Reading: Perceptual and Language Processes,* New York: Academic Press.

Senders, J. W., Fisher, D. F. and Monty, R. A. (1978) *Eye Movements and the Higher Psychological Functions,* Hillsdale, N.J.: Erlbaum.

Chapter 8

Ellis, A. W. (ed.) (1982) *Normality and Pathology in Cognitive Functions,* London: Academic Press.

Ellis, A. W. (1984) *Reading, Writing and Dyslexia: a Cognitive Analysis,* Hillsdale, N.J.: Erlbaum.

Index